The Book of
Strange and Curious
Legal Oddities

The Book of Strange and Curious Legal Oddities

Pizza Police, Illicit Fishbowls, and Other Anomalies of the Law That Make Us All Unsuspecting Criminals

Nathan Belofsky

A PERIGEE BOOK

A PERIGEE BOOK
Published by the Penguin Group
Penguin Group (USA) Inc.
375 Hudson Street, New York, New York 10014, USA
Penguin Group (Canada), 90 Eglinton Avenue East, Suite 700, Toronto, Ontario M4P 2Y3, Canada
(a division of Pearson Penguin Canada Inc.)
Penguin Books Ltd., 80 Strand, London WC2R 0RL, England
Penguin Group Ireland, 25 St. Stephen's Green, Dublin 2, Ireland (a division of Penguin Books Ltd.)
Penguin Group (Australia), 250 Camberwell Road, Camberwell, Victoria 3124, Australia
(a division of Pearson Australia Group Pty. Ltd.)
Penguin Books India Pvt. Ltd., 11 Community Centre, Panchsheel Park, New Delhi—110 017, India
Penguin Group (NZ), 67 Apollo Drive, Rosedale, North Shore 0632, New Zealand
(a division of Pearson New Zealand Ltd.)
Penguin Books (South Africa) (Pty.) Ltd., 24 Sturdee Avenue, Rosebank, Johannesburg 2196,
South Africa

Penguin Books Ltd., Registered Offices: 80 Strand, London WC2R 0RL, England

While the author has made every effort to provide accurate telephone numbers and Internet
addresses at the time of publication, neither the publisher nor the author assumes any
responsibility for errors, or for changes that occur after publication. Further, the publisher does not
have any control over and does not assume any responsibility for author or third-party websites or
their content.

Copyright © 2010 by Nathan Belofsky
Text design by Tiffany Estreicher

First edition: August 2010

Library of Congress Cataloging-in-Publication Data

Belofsky, Nathan.
   The book of strange and curious legal oddities : pizza police, illicit fishbowls, and other
anomalies of the law that make us all unsuspecting criminals / Nathan Belofsky.
      p.   cm.
   "A Perigee book"
   Includes bibliographical references and index.
   ISBN 978-0-399-53595-6
   1. Statutes—Humor.   I. Title.
   K183.B45   2010
   340—dc22   2010010647

PRINTED IN THE UNITED STATES OF AMERICA

10   9   8   7   6   5   4   3   2   1

Most Perigee books are available at special quantity discounts for bulk purchases for sales
promotions, premiums, fund-raising, or educational use. Special books, or book excerpts, can also
be created to fit specific needs. For details, write: Special Markets, Penguin Group (USA) Inc., 375
Hudson Street, New York, New York 10014.

Acknowledgments

A sincere thank-you to Sheree Bykofsky of Sheree Bykofsky Associates Inc. for introducing me to the publishing world, and to superagent Janet Rosen for thinking of me and then providing able representation. Finally, thanks to Maria Gagliano of Perigee for her keen insight and shaping of the manuscript, and to Erin Weinschenk for her administrative skills and creative contributions.

Contents

Introduction   ix

1. Old School   1

2. In the Neighborhood   57

3. Strange Things, Strange Places   75

4. Animals Among Us (The Real Ones)   85

5. Life's Essentials: Food and Sex   115

6. Entertainment and Leisure   145

7. People Getting Along   171

8. Judges, Lawyers, and the Law   195

Selected Bibliography   219

Index   235

Introduction

I'm a lawyer and this is a book about laws and, sometimes, the people who break them.

Most of the laws are strange, some silly, others infuriating, but all are chosen to be entertaining and thought provoking.

Some of the laws here we encounter every day, others concern issues we may never have even heard of. Many of the laws are old, from Babylonia and the Middle Ages and the Puritans, and some new, from the European Union and Flint, Michigan. The laws deal with snakes and sea cucumbers, death and injustice, cloud seeding and black holes, and virtually any other issue people or their lawgivers can devise.

It is my strong belief that real laws are far more interesting than made-up ones, so all the laws (and cases) in this book are real, not invented or misstated or exaggerated. You won't find a fictional law about tying alligators to fire hydrants or a ban on carrying an ice-cream cone in your back pocket, or any of the countless urban legends now recycled in dozens of books and on hundreds of Internet sites. The statutes here are almost always followed by legal citations, and those that aren't have been obtained from authoritative or scholarly works (a selected bibliography is included). And while I can't take credit for thinking up the laws, I am bringing many to the attention of the general public for the first time.

Along with the laws themselves, this book highlights the plight of regular people coping with real legal matters, some trivial, some life and death. I write of an English citizen who served months in jail for whistling the *Addams Family* song, and laws governing real estate brokers who sell haunted houses, and of the poor boy years ago who stole a flounced ditto and saw his life hang in the balance. And while the stories recounted here may serve to fascinate or entertain, we should never forget that these brushes with the law were quite real, and, to the people involved, often less than amusing.

Some of the laws here are just plain dumb, the result of accident or mistake, while others are borne of malice, the handiwork of petty (or real) dictators devoted to taking away our freedoms and our fun, and often enforced by bloated bureaucracies whose very survival depends on the creation of new and more laws. These laws regulate how fast ketchup must flow from the bottle and ban curvy cucumbers, and they tell us who can play dominoes and who can't.

Other strange laws made sense long ago but now serve only to provide a fascinating glimpse into times and cultures long past. The Sumerians regulated ox rentals; medieval tyrants, the stuffing of pillows; and the Puritans, just about everything—all may or may not have been right for their time, but they sure make great reading for ours.

Finally, there are more recent quirky laws, and these can be the most entertaining of all, illuminating as they do unusual lifestyles and questionable behaviors, some of them perhaps happening right down the street.

From studying the law over time we learn that customs and lifestyles come and go but people don't change—our greed, goodness, lust, and general foolishness march on. The Babylonians had their consumer protection statutes; the medieval Franks had laws against shooting poison arrows; and we have laws regulating the holes in cheese, animal cruelty, and boobie pillows. There's nothing new under the sun.

The people who write the laws haven't changed much, either. Modern Eurocrats would salute their Hittite brothers who carved minimum wage laws into stone tablets, and savvy Senate insiders would admire ancient Irish lawmakers for mandating how to distribute the bones of a whale. Likewise the lawmaking process itself: Today's legislators would surely appreciate the smoked-filled rooms where medieval lawmen decided whether *nose* should be inserted into the Maiming statute, or the arcane procedures of the Ordeal by Bread and Cheese.

The book can be read from cover to cover with ease, but is also designed for a quick dip, and for skipping around. So, for example, if you're not quite in the mood for some (very fun) history, read about horses or stink bombs or swill milk, and come back for the rest later.

Chapter 1 addresses ancient laws and ways of life, from libel to cross-dressing to the death penalty. Chapter 2 deals with newer and more familiar places and things, while Chapter 3 discusses matters a little more offbeat. Chapter 4 covers animals—how we use, abuse, protect, and even try them. Chapter 5 addresses life's basic needs (food and sex), and Chapter 6, what we do in our spare time. Chapter 7 discusses laws that govern how we get along with each other, or at least try to, and finally, Chapter 8 explores quirks of the legal establishment and the lawyers, judges, and bureaucrats who rule it, along with some of their strange rules and procedures.

In all, the book aims to give a unique and entertaining view of the strange side of our laws through the ages, and the people who've made and lived by them.

1

Old School

While the cavemen surely had their own primitive laws passed down through grunts and gestures, real legal history begins with the invention of writing, starting with stone tablets and papyrus and progressing to the miracle of the printing press. This chapter draws on these sources, covering laws from the ancient Egyptians to the Puritans.

A few common themes emerge: The Middle Ages were no picnic, rich was better than poor, men were better than women. Others aspects of ancient law seem almost random; over time, various societies became no more or less oppressive, their punishments neither harsher nor more lenient, their laws not more enlightened or less, just different.

But all of the legal rules here accurately reflect how ordinary people dealt with the law and vice versa, and how, legally or not, they worked, played, and made it through the day.

Don't Dent That Ox

Pursuant to the Sumerian Code of Lipit-Ishtar of about 1950 BCE, the following was legal compensation for damage to a rental ox:

- Eye: one-half retail value of ox.
- Flesh (at nose ring): one-third retail value of ox.
- Broken horn: one-quarter retail value of ox.
- Tail: one-quarter retail value of ox.

The Murder Act

Hanging by the neck till dead was too good a fate for British criminals, who were also subject to the Murder Act 1751 (25 Geo.2c37). The act mandated "that some further terror and peculiar mark of infamy be added to the punishment . . . and in no case whatsoever shall the body of any murderer be suffered to be buried."

The edict encouraged a ghoulish trade in dead bodies much desired by the curious surgeons and scientists of the day, who used them for dissection and in experiments, for better or worse reducing the number of bodies being publicly displayed in a gibbet or drawn and quartered and hung on spikes in the four quarters of the town. But it also fostered fierce competition among relatives trying to claim the bodies and body snatchers eager to sell them to doctors and surgeons.

George Foster drowned his wife and youngest son in a

canal. Like many a murderer, his hanged body was immediately carted off to a doctor. But unlike most, he was subjected by Professor Aldini, a pioneer in the mysterious properties of electricity, to the "galvanic process," in which bursts of electric current were run through his dead body. Proving the powers of galvanism to be beyond that of all others, in a scene witnessed by several people and carefully recounted in writing, Foster's jaw first quivered after a jolt of electricity, then an eye opened, then a hand clenched and raised itself. The raised hand then struck a witnessing beadle, a minor official of the Surgeons Company, who received such a shock that he died later that afternoon.

The father of a young woman named Mary Shelley was an acquaintance of Professor Aldini and spoke of his galvanism at the family dinner table. Ms. Shelley went on to write *Frankenstein, or The Modern Prometheus*, known more simply to generations of terrified book readers and moviegoers as *Frankenstein*.

Pleas of the Manor of Abbey (1200s): The entire township was punished for failing to wash the lord's sheep.

Babylmania

The Codex Hammurabi of Babylon is one of the oldest and the best known of the ancient law codes, dating back to approximately 1750 BCE. Discovered in 1901 by a French archaeologist in what is now Iran, the code consists of 282 laws and is inscribed on a seven-foot-tall stone slab now housed in the Louvre Museum in Paris.

The code mandated an eye for an eye (196), payment of one-third mina for knocking out a free man's tooth (201), sixty blows with an ox whip for striking one of higher rank (202), and impalement of a wife and her lover who killed a hapless husband (153).

The code also promoted strong family values. Women were protected from the evil of drink by being burned if found imbibing in a tavern (110), while a man who beat a free woman to death had to pay half a mina (212), the same as for cutting down a neighbor's tree (59). Killing maidservants was a relative bargain at one-third mina, and the anguished son of a prostitute who told his adopted father or mother that they were not his real parents had his tongue cut out (192).

The wisdom of the waters was paramount to Babylonian justice. An accused who leaped into the river and sank would give up possession of his house to his accuser, but if the river found the accused innocent, the accuser would be put to death and the accused would take his house (2). A wife who didn't pay attention to her housekeeping or her husband was cast into the water (143), a woman who abandoned her POW husband was thrown in the water (133), and a woman who cheated on her husband was thrown in the water tied to her lover (129). A woman accused of adultery but not caught sleeping with another man would be required to jump into the river for her husband (132).

The Codex Hammurabi had liberal consumer protection laws. If one rented an ox and it was killed in the field by a lion, the owner was forced to bear the loss (144). If a female bar manager told a patron she could not accept his corn for a drink and then billed him more than the value of the corn, she would be drowned (108). Fly-by-night contractors whose shoddy construction caused a house to collapse and kill its owner would themselves be killed (229); if the homeowner's son was caught in the collapse, the builder's innocent son would be put to death to make things even (230). A slip of the surgeon's knife causing injury required the chopping off of the doctor's hands (215), but the successful healing of a broken bone or "soft part" earned a doctor between 2 and 5 shekels (221–223).

Troublemaking Babylonians of means could avoid being cast in the water or otherwise inconvenienced by sharing their good fortune. A man who flooded his neighbor's land could smooth things over with ten gur of corn for every ten gan of land (57), while putting out the eye of another's slave cost just one-half mina (199), and using another's house to store one's own corn cost one gur for every five ka of corn per year (121). One caught stealing cattle or sheep or an ass or a pig or a goat would pay tenfold if the animal was owned by a freeman but a whopping thirtyfold if it "belong[ed] to a god." If all these penalties left the evildoer a bit light in the wallet and unable to pay, death would be the only alternative (8).

That Girl

From an ancient British manuscript recording the arrest and interrogation of one John Rykener in 1395, we learn that Mr. Rykener, calling himself Eleanor, was found dressed in women's clothing in a stall on Sopers Lane in

London, "committing that detestable unmentionable and ignominious vice." According to the confession, John Britby was passing along the high road of Cheap on Sunday and saw Rykener dressed as a woman. He agreed to pay Rykener, and they went to the stall together, where they were later arrested. Mr. Rykener revealed that his pimp was a certain Elizabeth Bronderer, who first thought to dress him in women's clothing and who, as a dutiful mother, also brought her daughter "to diverse men for the sake of lust."

Rykener also confessed that he practiced the "abdominable vice" on two Franciscan friars, Brother Michael and Brother John, who gave him a gold ring, and with two chaplains behind the Church of St. Margaret Pattens, and that he had sex with many nuns.

Tennis, Anyone?

We learn of everyday medieval village life from the Court Roll of Ramsey, England, a judicial account of various infractions by Ramsey townspeople. The document was drafted in 1460 on the Monday after the Feast of St. Anne, a celebration honoring the mother of the Virgin Mary, who, barren, was granted a child by an angel and dedicated her daughter to God's service. The citizens listed had to pay fines for their bad conduct (*d* is the abbreviation for a penny, and *s*, a shilling).

2d. from John Newman for having placed a dung heap too near the common lane.

6s., 8d. each from Thomas Porter, John Brothby, John Wytell and Peter Marche for putting dung near the Chapel St. Thomas.

6d. from John Faukes for assaulting Matthew Kelew.

6d. from the same John Faukes for assaulting Richard Merwyk and attempting to stab him with his dagger, and for throwing him into the river.

16d. from Thomas Plomer and 20 d. from John Asplond, bakers of bread, for selling bread contrary to the assize.

6d. each from John Brouse and William Wayte, ale-tasters, for not doing their job.

1d. each from Joan Brampton and Isabelle Stedeman, for not bringing their gallons and pottles before the steward.

6d. from William Stedeman for assaulting Thomas Wode and fracturing his skull.

6d. from Thomas Wode for unjustly raising the hue and cry on his wife, and from his wife for unjustly raising the hue and cry on him, which is something they do regularly, both day and night, to the great nuisance of their neighbors.

12d. from Robert Love, chaplain, for assaulting Thomas Love, his brother.

1d. from Katherine Love for unjustly raising the hue and cry on William Clerk.

A half-mark from William Warde for regularly having diverse men within his dwelling playing tennis, contrary to decree.

Frankly Absurd

Under the seventh-century Salic law of the German Franks, also called the Lex Salica, a Frank who shot a poison arrow but missed or hired an unsuccessful hit man paid a fine of 63 shillings, whereas a Frank who struck someone so hard that his brain and three bones above the brain were visible paid 30 shillings (Title XVII, §§ 1–3).

Raping a girl from the spinning room cost 63 shillings (Title XVIII, § 5). A Frank falsely calling a woman a harlot paid 45 shillings, but paid only 3 shillings for calling a woman a fox (Title XXX, §§ 3, 4).

Pyramid Scheme

Truly accurate accounts of the legal system of ancient Egypt are rare. Based mostly on broken tablets and indecipherable inscriptions, even those that can be understood are suspect, with scribes and officials often writing what they thought the gods wanted to hear.

Everyday accounts of routine court business are far more revealing. Like now, police armed with batons and sometimes accompanied by police dogs (and probably, more rarely, trained monkeys) patrolled the neighborhoods, and an elite cadre of detectives investigated crimes, often checking detailed public records and taking suspects to the riverbank for "questioning."

As is still the case today, schmoozing the local cop on the beat could cut a person a break. According to a scribe called Any from the New Kingdom (1500–1000 BCE), "Befriend the herald of your quarter, do not make him angry with you. Give him food from your house, do not slight his requests; say to him: 'Welcome, welcome here.' . . . No blame accrues to him who does it."

Criminal activity and suspects in ancient Egypt differed little from those of our own time, except in the particulars. According to a court memorandum of a theft published by Egyptologist Gaston Maspero, "workmen of Nakhu-m-Maut . . . went into my house, stole two large loaves and three cakes, spilt my oil, opened my bin containing the corn . . . stole half the killesteis [bread] . . . stole . . . eight sabu-cakes of Roshusu berries. . . . They drew a bottle of beer which was cooling in water." And extravagant Ari-Nofer, a resident of Thebes, went shopping and bought some slaves. When authorities suspicious of her husband's sudden wealth asked how she could make such a large purchase, Ari-Nofer responded that the money was hers. "I did not see the silver with which he paid their price. . . . I acquired it with the barley during the year of the hyaenas, when there was a famine." Ari-Nofer and her husband beat the rap.

Ancient Egyptian torts included adultery, eating sacred birds, and stealing food from the dead, and ultimate justice lay with the goddess Maat, who wore the feather of truth upon her head. Judges were chosen for their integrity, but those who proved otherwise were exiled to Tharu, a remote fortress town, or punished: During the Harem Conspiracy of Ramses III, appointees to a fourteen-member judicial panel were found to have partied down with harem women at the beer house and had their ears and noses cut off.

Punishment varied from restitution to banishment to death. Stealing a state-owned ox merited exile, while the servant of Pakhary the charioteer, who stole a bronze spittoon worth six deben, had to pay eighteen back, and fifty-one deben for a shirt of fine Upper Egyptian linen. Theft of hides was punishable by a hundred blows and five open sores. Death sentences were rare, but crimes against the state could merit impalement, burning at the stake, decapitation, being fed to Nile crocodiles, or—worst of all—denial of an afterlife.

The Judgment of the Pillory (1300s): Food purveyors found in violation of the Assize of Bread or otherwise cheating customers of their proper weight and measure faced a pillory of convenient strength or a tumbrel, trebuchet, or castigatory. The same fate awaited butchers and cooks who sold or seethed flesh and fish that had lost their wholesomeness, or those who bought the flesh of Jews and then sold it to Christians.

A Forest of His Own

The following are royal proclamations in effect in England in the late 1400s and early 1500s:

> A vagabond, idle or suspected person shall be put in the stocks for three days with only bread and water, and then put out of the town.

> No beasts may be slaughtered or cut up by butchers within the walls of the town . . . so that people will not be annoyed.

No tanner may be a currier . . . and no currier may be a tanner.

No longbow shall be sold for over the price of 3s, 4d.

No man may take eggs of any falcon, hawk or swan out of their nest.

Any person without a forest of his own who has a net device . . . to catch deer shall pay 200s for each month of possession.

Large salmon shall be sold without any small fish or broken-bellied salmon.

The herring shall be as good in the middle and in every part of the package as at the ends of the package.

The Laws Divine

During the starving time in 1610, England sent over the righteous Thomas Dale, a stern naval commander, to lead desperate British colonists in Virginia from darkness to light and from the deep pit of hell to the highest heaven.

On arrival, Dale was appointed deputy governor and found settlers eating dogs, cats, the leather of their boots and each other, and meanwhile idling and bowling in the streets. In response, Dale enacted the Lawes Divine, Morrall and Martiall, a strict criminal code exacting draconian penalties for even the most petty of crimes.

Twice a day church bells rang, and all had to report to services; those who didn't lost a day's wages for a first infraction and were whipped for a second. Those who didn't observe the Sabbath received the same punishment and were executed for a third infraction, and a person who murmured or mutinied against government officials begged forgiveness on his knees while being whipped, with a second offense bringing service aboard a ship or perhaps a hot needle through the tongue.

Ravishing a woman, even if a maid or an Indian, brought death, and adulterers were whipped; an adulterer caught a third time asked public forgiveness at the Assembly and was whipped three times a week for a month anyway. Women guilty of sexual misdeeds were required to wear white gowns and stand on chairs during public worship, holding a white wand.

Any man that owned or borrowed a tool had to have it registered in his name, and one who stole or even just broke or lost a spade, shovel, hatchet, or ax was whipped, while a person stealing clothing, tools, shoes, hats, or linen was to be executed, as was one who plucked from a garden or farm or vineyard a root or flower or ear of corn that wasn't his.

A baker who stole a loaf or deceived with weight or measure or made the bread coarser on purpose and kept the flour for himself had his ears cut off; the same fate awaited cooks who seethed flesh and then made less for others by cutting away for themselves, or expected something back in return for ladling out bigger portions. On penalty of same, dressers of sturgeon had to give a just and true account of their wares.

Pleas at Northampton (1200s): Neighbors complained that Geoffrey took from every cart of eels crossing his land one stick of eels and from every cart of greenfish one greenfish and from every cart of herrings five herrings. Geoffrey said he was entitled to it as landowner and requested a court ruling.

Red Menace

Ancient Russia's Russkaya Pravda was compiled in the eleventh and twelfth centuries and governed civil and criminal law. Its successor, the Sudebnik, was written in about 1500.

Under the Sudebnik, some civil cases were tried by judicial duel, supervised by court administrators. A defendant who was too old or small or was a nun or a woman could hire someone to fight in his or her place, but fans and supporters were barred from bringing armor, sticks, or oak clubs.

Pursuant to the Pravda, tax collectors on their route were entitled to seven buckets of malt, a ram, or two nogatas and, on Wednesdays, either one rezena or a ration of cheese, plus two chickens daily. Their page boys received twelve squirrel pelts when they finished the job.

Under the Sudebnik, a thief caught stealing for the first time would be punished with the knout, a multiple whip made of rawhide and sometimes metal or wire hooks, or a great knout, soaked in milk and dried in the sun to make it harder. First-timers would also pay a fine and make recompense, and if they couldn't, they'd serve as the victim's slave. Stealing another person's slave cost 12 grivnas, and a prince's beehive 3, but theft of a dove cost only 9 kunas.

Under the Pravda, if a person hit another with a stick or bowl or drinking horn he paid 12 grivnas, and assaulting someone's mustache cost 12; a person torturing a slave paid 3. A man who pushed or pulled another in front of witnesses was fined 3 grivnas, but if the victim was a Varangian, the Varangian would have to take an oath to ensure he was telling the truth about the incident. Killing a caretaker cost 80 grivnas and a stable boy, 40, but if one killed a woman or smerd or zakup, the fine was just 5 or 6 grivnas.

Time After Time

[P]ardon and acquite all and euery prest as well religious as seculer for all manner of rape done.
—Petition of Commons That Priests Be Pardoned for All Accusations of Rape (1449)

No Guns for Jews

Pursuant to Ireland's Assize of Arms (1191), "let every holder of a knight's fee have a hauberk [shirt of mail armor], a helmet, a shield and a lance." The law was drafted to ensure that citizens could defend their country in case of invasion.

The statute, which is now in the process of being abolished, specifically prohibited Jews from owning a coat of mail or hauberk and is commonly thought to have barred Jews from owning weapons as well.

The law apparently has an enthusiastic following in America. Stormfront.org, a white supremacy group ("White Pride World Wide"), cites the statute on its website, with the part concerning Jews in boldface, and a 1982 Report of the Senate Judiciary Committee, prefaced by Senator Orrin Hatch, cited the 1181 statute to support the Right to Bear Arms and to defeat pending gun control legislation.

Putting on the Ritz

An invited guest would have his right hand cut off during a sophisticated soiree held especially in his honor, courtesy of Stat. 33 Henry VIII, Ch. 12.

The statute was applied to those found guilty of malicious striking and bloodshed in the king's household, and was apparently designed to teach the staff manners. The affair was invitation only, with white glove service and the very finest in food, wine, linen, and cutlery.

Pursuant to the statute, the sergeant of the pantry would serve bread and the sergeant of the poultry a chicken to the honored guest (ix, xiv), and the sergeant of the cellar a pot of red wine (x). The sergeant of the ewry would run linen service to soak up the blood (xi), and the master cook would bring the utensils to cut the chicken up and the hand off (xiii). A surgeon would be on hand to wrap the stump (xiv).

Sir Edmund Knyvet was a guest of honor, and a brief account details his experience with "a new form of punishment"; after the cock's head was cut off and ale and beer brought from the cellar, Knyvet humbly confessed his guilt and asked that his left hand be cut off instead of his right. The king heard his plea and, after learning of his gentle nature from the Lords and Ladies, issued him a pardon. Others were surely not so lucky.

Upside-Down Tricks and Crisscross Maneuvers

In medieval China, men learned in the law were prohibited from representing others involved in court proceedings, and courts did what they could to crack down on shady "legal tricksters." But powerless and illiterate citizens often needed someone to confront their adversaries or even the authorities themselves; this challenge to authority, as well as legitimately bad behavior, is a factor in many decisions and related documents collected in the book *The Enlightened Judgments: Ch'ing-Ming Chi—The Sung Dynasty Collection.*

Trickster Mr. Chang was a major player around the courthouse and determined whether legal-related matters were "upside down or inside out," according to court records. Chang was clever, exploiting every loophole, and a crook, forging legal documents and bribing officials. On the day of his arrest he had cut the line, according to legal accounts, and "the four to five hundred people who had been standing along the two corridors waiting to submit documents gave a thunderous and happy cheer." Chang confessed to swindles amounting to fifty strings of coins, surely only a tiny percentage of his crimes, and he was sentenced to fifteen strokes on the back, a tattoo on the face, and prison.

Trickster Lung Tuan was in the habit of involving himself in noisy litigations and loaning money to court personnel to gain their influence. When he violated a ban on loans to the military by lending to the archers, he was sentenced to eighty strokes with the heavy rod. But he was then found to be a scholar, and his sentence reduced to fifteen strokes with a bamboo grid.

A devout Taoist beat another man to death and was sued for wrongful death by the victim's relatives. A trickster named Lou persuaded the plaintiff to amend his pleadings to exaggerate the economic damages, hammered out a secret private settlement, and then had the body cremated to avoid further investigation. The court wrote:

> [W]hat he did was . . . upside down tricks and crisscross maneuvers. . . . [I]t has become customary to engage noisily in litigation. It is not that the people themselves really like to litigate, rather it has to do with a layer of rootless agitators. Having neither other abilities nor any occupation, they litigate to gain their livelihood. They run after what is rank; they seek out what is scarred and dirty. . . . [T]heir wishes will determine whether it goes straight or sideways. The gains go to them and the disasters by the common people.

Lou was sentenced to thirteen strokes and imprisoned for one and a half years.

According to the judge, Peng was nothing more than an illiterate village rustic, and all his crafty court maneuverings were taught to him by legal trickster Hsien, whom he trusted, as did other innocents, who saw someone with a big mouth and a long tongue. If Peng and others were lucky enough to win their lawsuit, all the gains would go to the trickster, the court said, and if they lost, the disaster was their own. "I am as deeply resentful of [law tricksters] as I am of noxious odors," wrote the judge, who, for representing Peng, sentenced Hsien to one hundred strokes, and put him on public display at the marketplace.

Mr. Chao was a respected village citizen but with a rank as low as that of an ant, and one could easily imagine him acting like a fox in the city and a rat in the temple, the court said. Chao was nonetheless the person unsophisticated villagers sought out when involved in court proceedings, hiring him to stand up for their rights.

When three monks retained him, the irked judge said he couldn't punish Chao, since that would be like cracking the whip on the cart to startle the ox. He instead sentenced each of the three monks to a hundred strokes, prison, and public display with a cangue around their neck.

Trickster Cheng pursued legal cases aggressively; he spent every day standing at the door of the district office chasing business, and when he heard of people who were about to be served or arrested, he would rush to their homes and offer his services. Using devilish tricks, the court said, he would hold the hands of those who had money and show the door to those who didn't, and charge fees until his clients became bankrupt.

In a property dispute, Cheng invited a witness subpoenaed by the court to meet his client, the person against whom he was testifying, for drinks at his home . . . at the very time the witness was supposed to appear in court. When court officers came knocking, Cheng hid the witness and then allowed him to escape out the back door. Cheng received one hundred strokes.

The Extermination of the Clan McGregor

The McGregors were a troublesome bunch, continuously engaged in blood feuds over land and hunting rights in the forest. So in 1603 Scotland's Privy Council passed the Edict for the Extermination of the Clan Gregor, 1603. Feb. 24:

> [A]s the wicked and unhappie race of Clangregour . . .
> hes continewit in bluid, thift, sorning, and oppresssioun
> upoun the peciable and guid subjectis of the incuntrey,
> to the wraik miserie, and undoing of mony honest and
> substantious hous halderis . . . in maist barbarous and
> horrible maner, without pitie or compassion, they have
> murdreist and slane. . . . God can not be appeasit . . .
> unless that unhappie and destable race be extirpat and
> Ruttit out.

The McGregor problem was long-standing, but the most egregious incident occurred in 1598, when some McGregors, along with some McDonalds, killed John Drummond, a king's forester who had cut off some McGregor ears as punishment for poaching. They then paid a visit to Drummond's unsuspecting pregnant sister, Margaret, who gave her guests an appetizer and went to prepare dinner; upon coming back to the group, she was met with the sight of her brother's head on the table, its mouth stuffed with bread and cheese.

More edicts followed, with bounties placed: McGregor men were hanged and McGregor women and children were sold into slavery. Acts against the McGregors were finally repealed, and the McGregor name was restored in 1774, nearly two hundred years later.

The Bawdy Courts

During the 1600s and 1700s, British churches supervised a justice system parallel to that of the government, with quasi-religious tribunals called Bawdy Courts responsible for punishing whoredom, adulterous criminal conversation, and assorted frivolity and horseplay.

Lawrence Heath was punished for showing up drunk in church, and in 1608 thirty-five people were cited for watching football when they should have been at services.

Elizabeth "Few Clothes" Smyth was ticketed for committing adultery with two men, one a wizard, while defendant Walter Garlick boasted that he could have fourteen women at his pleasure. Clergyman Thomas Holden was accused of drinking, brawling, and whoring, while Agnes Ridge was sanctioned for throwing rocks at her mother-in-law.

Tragedy occurred in 1630, when blacksmith Thomas Richardson and his hooligans picked the lock of the church belfry and for three weeks rang the bells each evening, sometimes very late. Some young maidens joined in the fun, and one got tangled up in the ropes, thrown on her head, and put in a coma.

Ann Jillman of London gave birth to an illegitimate child and sought forgiveness. Redemption was granted when she kneeled at the front of the church wearing a white sheet, listening to a sermon denouncing her, and holding a white rod in her hand.

Charlemagne the Pious

King Charlemagne, who forcibly converted the Saxons to Christianity in central and western Europe, was among the most devout of rulers; he was briefly anointed a saint, although his canonization was later annulled. Son of Pippin the Short, Charlemagne was said to have been seven times one foot tall. In 1861 his tomb was opened and his skeleton measured by scientists, who found him to be six feet three inches, still enormous for his time.

Charlemagne's Capitulary for Saxony (775–790 CE) is a law code substantially devoted to issues of faith and worship, and he expressed his love for God by ordering the execution of those who ate meat during Lent (Art. 4) or cremated a dead body instead of burying it (Art. 7) or scorned a baptism (Art. 8).*

One paid the ultimate price by consorting with the devil and sacrificing an innocent man to the demons

*Doing penance with a sympathetic priest *might* save one from execution.

(Art. 9), as did a person who was deceived by the devil into believing that a woman was a witch who ate men and as a result burned the woman and gave her flesh to others to eat, or ate it himself (Art. 6).

A Day in the Life . . .

May 27, 1606, was a busy day for the British House of Lords, which proposed, considered, noted, accepted, rejected, or expedited the following acts:

Act for the Better Preservation of Sea Fish

Act to Reform the Multitudes and Misdemeanors of Attorneys and Solicitors at Law, and to Avoid Sundry Unnecessary Suits and Charges in Law

Act for the True Making of Woollen Cloth

Act Against Unlawful Hunting and Stealing of Deer and Conies

Act for the Reformation of the Common Sin of Swearing

Act for the Better Discovering and Repressing of Popish Recusants

Act to Put Down the Multitudes of Unnecessary Brokers and to Avoid the Occasion of Infinite Idleness and Stealths

Act for Prohibiting All Such from Brewing of Beer and Ale

Act for the Better Explaining of a Former Act

Act to Restrain the Transportation of Coloured Cloths Undrest

Act Against the Loathsome Sin of Drunkenness

Act Against Scandalous and Unworthy Ministers

Act for the Abating, and to Restrain, the New Erection
    of Wears, Stanks, Kiddles, and Other Obstructions

Act to Restrain Abuses of Players

Lex Loco

The Lex Frisionum was a compilation of French and German laws written in the time of Charlemagne, roughly 750 CE, and may have been in effect for hundreds of years before that.

Although secular in nature, the laws were heavily influenced by the church, sometimes to odd effect.

For example, if a man was killed during a riot and the killer was lost among the crowd, a reward seeker could accuse seven men of manslaughter. Each would give a twelve-fold oath that he was innocent, then be led to a church, where lots would be drawn, two of which would be a broken willow twig, one of them marked with the sign of the cross. The lots would then be wrapped in pure wool, and one would be chosen by a priest or innocent boy. If the marked lot was chosen, all seven would be let go; if not, each accused would mark a lot with his own sign and the priest or innocent boy would choose them one by one, with the owner of the last drawn lot deemed guilty (Lex 2, Title XIV).

But despite church influence the laws are most notable for their scientific certitude, with nearly every possible human wrong redressed through the application of precise mathematical formulas.

A nobleman accidentally killing a fellow nobleman paid 80 solidi, but only 53 for killing a freeman and 27 for a serf (Lex 1, Title I). The price for anyone killing a slave was subject to the offender's honest discretion, the same as for killing of a sow or swine (Lex 1, Title IV). One who killed a hawk dog or beagle was fined 4 solidi, and a dog that could kill a wolf 3, and a watchdog 1, but a dog "that does not do anything but only hangs around in the court and in the house" was worth a mere 1 tremisse (Lex 1, Title IV). Cutting off a person's mustache earned a 4-solidi fine (Lex 4, Add. III, Additions of the Wise Men), while a person who hit a harp player paid a fine one-quarter more than that for hitting someone who didn't play the harp (Lex 4, Add. III, Additions of the Wise Men).

Not everything was so costly—a person killing an arsonist was let off for free, as was a mother who starved or strangled her newborn baby (Lex 1, Title V).

A huge part of the Lex is occupied by the classification of wounds. A wound as long as the distance between the thumb and index finger cost 8 solidi, from elbow to tip of thumb 18, and from elbow to fingertips 24 (Lex 3, Ch. XXII). A blow to the face that caused a mutilation that could be seen from twelve feet was worth 3 times 4 solidi (Lex 4, Add. III, Additions of the Wise Men). If a piece of lung or some intestine came through a wound, one paid an extra 4 solidi in addition to the cost of the wound itself, and if a sword touched a person's brain membrane, the price would be 18 solidi, rising to 24 if the brain leaked out (Lex 3, Ch. XXII). If a bone came out of a wound that was so big that when thrown over a public road onto a shield one could hear the sound of it, an extra 4 solidi was assessed, while less noisy bones were assessed half that (Lex 3, Ch. XXII).

Sex under Lex was also by the numbers. Touching the breast of a free woman cost 4 solidi (Lex 3, Title 22), while he who fornicated with another man's slave that neither milked nor grinded had to pay 12 (Lex 2, Title VIII), and kidnapping and dishonoring a virgin girl could cost between 10 and 30 solidi (Lex 1, Title IX). A man who violated a virgin slave paid 4 solidi, but if she had been previously raped he paid just 3, and if he was the third to rape her, only 3, and if the fourth, just 1 (Lex 1, Title IX).

The Malefactor's Bloody Register

To British families of the 1700s and 1800s, reading the *Newgate Calendar* (subtitled *The Malefactor's Bloody Register*) was almost as edifying as attending an execution in person. Originally compiled from pamphlets passed out at hangings, the volumes, along with the Bible and *The Pilgrim's Progress*, were found in most decent British homes. The books chronicled the lives and usually deaths of those accused of crimes, and children especially were encouraged to learn from their examples. One edition has a picture of a young boy being handed a copy by his beaming mother, who gently points at a body hanging just outside the window.

The various editions tell the stories of a thousand or so accused criminals, many but not all hanged.

Joseph Wood and Thomas Underwood. Both fourteen years old and part of a gang of pickpockets and footpads, they robbed a twelve-year-old of a jacket, shirt, and waistcoat and then beat him. They refused an offer of mercy in return for implicating their companions and were hanged on July 6, 1791.

Molly Cutpurse. Born Mary Frith, Molly was a tomrig who liked to dress in men's clothes, wear a doublet, and smoke a pipe. She associated with roaring men, made a living as a pickpocket and pimp, and may have been burned in the hand for thievery. It is certain that she was arrested for indecent dress and prostitution in 1611 and forced to do penance. Ms. Cutpurse eventually settled down to sell stolen goods in a pawnshop and lived comfortably into old age.

John Williamson. An industrious shoemaker and widower, Williamson fell in love with a wealthy but mentally disabled woman, whom he confined to a closet, tied up, and starved for a month. He savagely beat a little girl who gave her a stool and some food. The woman died a day after being released, and Williamson was executed on January 19, 1767. His orphaned children were taken to the Cripplegate Workhouse.

Amos Merritt. Convicted of foot robbery, Patrick Maden was on the gallows with the cart underneath when Merritt stepped forward from the crowd and declared Maden innocent. After an hour of confusion during which the other condemned were left with ropes around their necks, Merritt confessed to the crime and Maden was released. A year later, after stealing a gold watch, Merritt was hanged in the very same spot, on January 10, 1775.

Francis Smith. For weeks women walking near the cemetery in the Hammersmith neighborhood just outside of London were accosted by an apparition, the Ghost of Hammersmith. Smith, normally a mild man of generous temper, lay in wait for the ghost and shot and killed bricklayer Thomas Millwood, who was dressed in his usual work uniform of white trousers and a white apron. A jury convicted Smith of manslaughter, but Lord Byron demanded a verdict of either murder or acquittal, with no compromise. Found guilty of murder and sentenced to die the next Monday, Smith received a reprieve and served one year.

Ann Marrow. Dressed as a man, Ms. Marrow would ensnare love-starved women and then steal their money. In 1777, she was sentenced to three months in prison and one stand on the pillory at Charing Cross. Great was the resentment of female spectators, who pelted her to such a degree that she was blinded in both eyes.

Henry Goodiff. A headstrong youth, Goodiff ran away from home. While rambling about, he encountered a knavish pastry peddler who cheated boys and girls and country clowns. After being swindled by the rogue, Goodiff went too far in seeking redress and was sentenced to die. A pardon was granted on condition that he serve in the navy, but he stubbornly refused and insisted that his original death sentence be carried out. His parents dragged the willful boy to a ship on the Thames and hurriedly pressed him into Her Majesty's Court Service.

Pleas—The Hundred of Triggshire (1200s): Lucy of Morwinstow claimed that three boys robbed her of 20 shillings and a cloak, but jurors believed otherwise, finding that Lucy was actually a hireling who laid down with a man in the garden; when the boys hooted her, she left her cloak, and the boys pawned it for two gallons of wine.

Through the Looking Glass

St. Patrick (circa 390–460) may have driven the snakes out of Ireland, but he wisely left the Emerald Isle's lively legal traditions behind. From the Brehan Law (from the Gaelic *breitheamhan*, meaning "judge"), a tradition of oral jurisprudence, St. Patrick supervised the creation of the *Senchus Mor* and related volumes, which detailed written laws and legal opinions.

The colorfully worded legal commentaries sometimes read like a passage from *Alice in Wonderland*; one charming note seems to describe the penalty for stealing services from a weaver: "for the ornamented thread, for the looking-glass which one woman besews from another, for the black-and-white cat, for the lap-dog of a queen."

Likewise, the actual laws have an air of unreality. Most unusually, people of higher rank who transgressed were often punished more severely than those of lower rank, and one who was owed a debt would collect by sitting on the stoop of the debtor and fasting, knowing that if he starved to death the debtor would be charged with murder, if he didn't die of embarrassment first.

There were fines for stumbling bishops and for fraudulent poets and for carrying off bond maids, and for stealing bees from an herb garden. One could not take fat and skinny pigs and sheep without wool or keep animals that scraped. Fines were collected for wearing down hatchets, for scaring the timid, for carrying a boy into a house on one's back so that the boy struck his head against the doorway, and for stripping the bark off a tree.

There were crimes of hand and crimes of foot, and rules to protect the "woman with the fetid breath," and the "lepress," and the "shriveled woman without juice." One who took a child's toys, "those goodly things which remove dullness from little boys," had to give them back in one day.

A doctor's office had to be in a proper house, clean and without dirty snails, with water running through the middle, and with four open doors—one on each side, so people could see in. The sick person would have to be protected from women, dogs, and fools.

The morsel always belonged to the champion, but the longed-for morsel craved by a pregnant woman could not be withheld by her husband, although a charmed morsel could be given to the dog to prove an enchantment.

There were rules about distributing the bones of a whale. And always to be kept on the fire was a cauldron and even a great cauldron for unexpected guests, with the haunch reserved for the king, bishop, and literary doctor; the leg for the chief; the head for the charioteer; and the steak for the queen. A hotel keeper had to own a cauldron big enough to accommodate a pig and a cow together.

A feller of trees had to remove all beasts and the blind and sleeping people before the first blow of the ax, and the fine for a hen's trespass into a neighbor's garden was one oat cake plus a side dish of butter or bacon.

These gentle laws remained in effect for nearly twelve hundred years.

Act Infinitim

The following are British acts that were passed and in effect in England for hundreds of years:

Act for the True Making of Pynnes [Pins] (1543)

Act Against the Killing of Beasts Called Weanlings (1532)

Act for Suppressing the Detestable Sin of Incest, Adultery and Fornication (1650)

Heron's Fish-Curing Patent Void Act (1623)

Horsebread Act (1540 and 1623)

Widows Bequest of Corn on Her Land Act (1235)

He Is a Bastard That Is Born Before the Marriage of His Parents Act (1235)

Act for Burying in Woollen (1677)

Act to Restrain All Persons from Marriage Until Their Former Wives and Former Husbands Be Dead (1604)

Act for Preventing the Mischiefs and Dangers That May Arise by Certain Persons Called Quakers . . . (1661)

Act Against Unlawful and Deceitful Stuffing and Making of Featherbeds (1551)

Stealing Hawk's Eggs Act (1540)

Worsted Yarn Act (1541 and 1547)

Abstinence from Flesh Act (1548)

Gads of Steel Act (1548)

Slaughter of Beasts Act (1483)

Act Concerning Outlandish People Calling Themselves Egyptians (1530)

What an Ordeal!

Justice during the reign of England's King Athelstan (924–939 CE) relied on an infallible combination of God and science. An accused would be surrounded on each side by an equal number of men who had fasted and been abstinent from their wives for the night and who had tasted of the holy water and kissed the image of Christ's rood.

If the test be by iron, the accused would go unto the iron and carry it nine feet, from stake to mark. If by boiling water, or brass or lead, one accused of a single crime would dip the hand to grab the stone up to the wrist, but if the accusation be threefold then up to the elbow.

Afterward, the hand would be swathed with bandages and inspected three days later; whether clean or foul would indicate innocence or guilt.

A more pleasing alternative was the Ordeal by Bread and Cheese, recorded in the text of a medieval church Mass, during which a carefully rationed weight of bread and cheese was given to the suspect, the bread unleavened and made of barley, and the cheese made in the month of May from the milk of ewes. At the altar, while Mass was being said, the suspect would be watched to see if he was able to swallow the large morsel and was thus innocent, with the corners of his mouth pressed by inspectors to ensure that he contrived no trick.

By the middle of the thirteenth century, these crude procedures were substantially replaced by a more just and sophisticated judicial device—torture—a technique used by certain of our most advanced nations even today.

Close Shave

When Russia's Peter the Great came to power in 1696, one of his top legislative priorities was the elimination of beards.

Beards were either banned outright or the subject of stiff taxes. Besides finding them to be a "ridiculous ornament," the autocratic Peter was intent on westernizing Russian society, and the elimination of feudal-looking beards was felt to be an important first step. Clean-cut mustaches were allowed.

Peter felt so strongly about the issue that he personally cut, or possibly even yanked, the beards off his noblemen. He is also said to have taken pride in personally yanking the teeth of those who complained of a toothache.

In the following years, Peter became known for imposing more and more taxes: on beehives, candles, nuts, boots, hats, horses, and chimneys. By 1724, his most infamous tax, the "soul tax"—a tax on Russian males for merely existing—made up over 50 percent of the government budget.

Render unto Caesar

Under the Twelve Tables, a body of legislation that stood as the foundation of Roman law, Rome in 500 BCE boasted the most sophisticated judiciary system of its time.

A plaintiff was obliged to provide an aged or infirm defendant a team of oxen with which to get to court, although a plaintiff wasn't required to "spread a carriage with cushions" for the comfort of his adversary if he didn't want to (I-3).

Witnesses were encouraged to be truthful, and those who weren't were flung from the Tarpeian Rock (VIII-23). Enchanting or singing an evil incarnation that dishonored another brought death (VII-1a, 1b), while breaking another's limb earned retaliation in kind or a penalty of 300 asses (VII-2, 3). Stealing crops or pastureland warranted sacrifice to Ceres (VI-9), and a person who burned a stack of grain beside someone's house would be bound, scourged, and burned to death himself (VII-10).

One who owed money was granted thirty days to pay before being summoned to court (Table III-1), and if unable to pay, he was taken by his creditor and bound with a thong of not less than fifteen pounds in weight (III-3). A creditor would then have to feed his debtor a pound of grits daily (III-4), and if a settlement wasn't procured, the debtor would be held in bonds for sixty days, brought to the meeting place on three successive market days, and then, at the creditor's whim, sold into slavery across the Tiber River or cut into pieces (II-5).

The Book of Dooms

Under *The Book of Dooms*, first drafted by English's King Ethelberht in the late sixth century, money talked and those who had it walked, with no mention in the *Dooms* of prison or exile or death for even the most serious of crimes. Cash, precisely calibrated, was what counted.

One slaying a nobleman's cupbearer paid 12 shillings (§ 14), while killing a freeman cost 50. The four front teeth went for 6; the teeth next to them, 4; the teeth next to those, 3; and then a shilling apiece (§ 51). A struck-off thumb cost 20 shillings; a thumbnail, 3; shooting finger, 8; middle finger, 4; ring finger, 6; little finger, 11; and each fingernail, 1 (§ 54).

Cold calculation prevailed in even the most personal of matters. Laying with a freeman's wife was settled by giving the jilted husband a large payment and a spare woman (§ 31); if one carried off someone else's maiden, he paid 50 shillings and bought the owner someone he liked almost as much (§ 82). An honest trade of cattle for a maiden was final, but returns were allowed if the deal was found to be the product of guile (§ 77).

Even the king himself apparently preferred shillings to sentiment: One could lay with the king's maiden for 50 shillings and live to tell about it (§ 10); laying with a grinding slave cost 25, and laying with a third class just 12 (§ 11).

Pleas at Lichfield (1200s): L. was suspected of involvement in Reinild's death and was ordered to undertake the ordeal of the iron, but she was feeling under the weather and the ordeal was delayed until she felt better.

Commune of Biella

Communes thrived in northern Italy from the 1100s. Walled city-states with their own armies, they maintained security from outside invaders through discipline within their own walls, as illustrated by the Statutes of the Commune of Biella, in effect from the twelfth century to the 1600s.

New appointees to the consulate had to buy fellow members one "good" free lunch and lost their entire salary and paid a stiff weekly fine until the lunch was bought (5). Members of the Credenzia who didn't come when the bells rang had to pay a fine (45), as did nuns who didn't mark the third hour with the ringing of the bell to assemble the poor (90).

It was forbidden to maintain a cooperage next to the fish traps (184), but taxes would not be imposed on people coming from the Forum on Wednesdays, except on those who were thieves, brigands, and rapists (66). Harnessing an oxen could be done only during the day (207), and one who kept lambs during the forbidden times paid 5 solidi (211).

Keeping a willow tree within the walls of the city was banned (212), and garbage couldn't be left in the area beginning at the baker's oven and ending at the home of Jacob the Jew (187). All homeowners had to have rain gutters, which were to be cleaned out periodically (192), and a person climbing atop a church paid a fine of 20 solidi (73).

Up to Code

In ancient Assyria under the Code of Assura (circa 1075 BCE), the war between the sexes was no contest at all—the woman always lost.

Unless otherwise forbidden in the tablets, a man could strike his wife, or pull her hair, or bruise her ear, and he would commit no misdeed (§ I.58), while a woman who struck a man received twenty blows and a fine of thirty manas of lead (§ I.7); a woman who kicked a man where it hurts had one of her fingers cut off, and her eyes plucked out if both testicles were lost (§ 1.8). In fairness, a woman was allowed to engage in low talk against her husband since she was only bringing shame upon herself (§ 1.2), and a man who brought his hand against another man's wife and treated her like a little child had one of his own fingers cut off; if he kissed her, the blade of an ax would be drawn down on his lower lip (§ I.9).

Pregnant women, or more accurately their fetuses, were highly valued—"If a man strike the wife of a man, in her first stage of pregnancy, and cause her to drop that which is in her, it is a crime; two talents of lead he shall pay" (§ 150); "If a man strike a harlot and cause her to drop that which is in her, blows for blows they shall lay upon him; he shall make restitution for a life" (§ I.51). *Choice* was not an option in ancient Assyria; a woman who lost a pregnancy of her own accord would be crucified, not buried (§ I.52).

A man who raped a married woman, whom he thought to be single, on a highway or in a hotel by mistake was excused and would go free; however, when the woman got home, her distraught husband would be free to do with her as he liked (§ I.14). But if the wife of a man was walking on the highway and another man seized her and said, "I will surely have intercourse with you" and she defended herself, the man would be put to death (§ I.12).

A man and woman caught fooling around by a husband could be put to death by the state or the husband could kill his wife on his own, although if he did so, he'd also have to put the man to death. And if he merely cut off his wife's nose, he had to turn the man into a eunuch (§ I.15). Meanwhile, a man falsely bragging to a companion that he had slept with his wife would get forty blows, work for the king for a month, pay 1 talent of lead, and be mutilated (§ I.18).

Property other than women also received close attention under the code. A buyer wishing to close on a house cleared title to the land by traveling to the city of Ashur, and "three times in a month," pronouncing his intent to buy the "Field and House of So and So," so that anyone asserting a claim on the property could bring his tablets before the magistrates and prove his rights to the disputed title (§ II.6).

More ordinary dealings were also addressed. A man meddling with his neighbor's field would receive one hundred blows, pay threefold, and lose the fingers of his hands. Those caught selling the children of others would get one hundred lashes and lose their money and their last-born son (§ III.2), while men and woman practicing sorcery who were caught red-handed would be put to death (§ I.47).

The Hittites of Hatti

The Nesilin Code (1750 BCE) governed the earlier of the Hittite civilizations in what is now Turkey.

One who injured a man would send someone to his house to take care of him, pay him 6 half shekels of silver, and pay the doctor bills (§ 10). Causing a woman to miscarry in her fifth month cost 5 half shekels; in the tenth month, 10 half shekels.

Stealing or maiming slaves could be troublesome; although one caught swiping a Luwian from western Turkey would just have to give him back (§ 21), one who stole a Nesian-speaking Hittite and led him to the land of Hatti had to pay the owner 12 shekels (§ 20). Even just blinding a slave could be costly, at 10 half shekels (§ 8). And an ungrateful slave who set a house on fire had his nose and ears cut off and given back to his master (§ 99), while one who rose against his master was put in a pit (§ 173).

Minimum wage and price controls for goods and services were enforced to the shekel. A man who bound sheaves, loaded them onto carts, and spread them onto the straw barn for three months was to receive thirty pecks of barley (§ 158), and one harnessing a yoke to an ox was entitled to a half peck. A smith earned one hundred pecks of barley for a copper box (§ 160), and a great cow sold for seven and a half (§ 178). A tub of lard or two cheeses cost a half peck, and buying an artisan's apprentice cost 10 half shekels (§ 176).

Domestic relations laws were strict but fair. Having intercourse with a pig or dog earned a death sentence, but a person doing the same with a horse or mule was let free, as long as he kept his distance from the king and didn't become a priest (§ 199). If an innocent person was sprung upon and sexually assaulted by an ox or a pig, the animal would be killed (although not eaten) and the person let free (§ 199).

In more traditional romantic relationships, a man raping a woman in the mountains would be killed, but if he raped her in a house the woman was killed (§ 197). A swinger who picked up "now this woman, now that one, now in this country, then in that country" was not subject to punishment (§ 191), nor were brothers sleeping with free women, one after the other or together, or fathers and sons doing the same with slaves and harlots (§ 194).

Pushy neighbors were treated with a firm hand; those who came over to borrow but then picked a quarrel and threw down their bread or their wine jug had to give their hosts one sheep, ten loaves, and some beer, and then promise not to show up on their doorstep for a full year (§ 164).

The Pleas of the Crown

The Pleas of the Crown record English cases arising in the 1200s. Many if not most involved death, either through accident or homicide; the majority of homicides grew out of disputes between people well known to each other. Those not involving death out of anger or intention were usually declared "misadventures." Upon a finding of misadventure, the value of the thing or animal involved in the accident, the "deodand," would be offered to God.

On the Sunday before the Nativity, Richard went to a wrestling match and got into a quarrel. From above, Amulf the monk threw a stone and crushed him to death. Amulf the monk fled and was deemed a fugitive.

Cecily and her maid Juliana got into a fight and both women fell into a leaden vessel of boiling water, scalding them to death. Misadaventure was found and the vessel valued at 4 shillings. Misadventure was also found when Nicholas fell from a pear tree.

On the morrow of the Assumption, William played chess with Robert, son of Bernard the Knight, and during an argument William stabbed Robert, took sanctuary in a church, and fled. Richard also fled, after accidentally hitting Walter in the head with an arrow while practicing with his crossbow.

One-year-old-Amice was bitten by a sow and died; the sow was valued at 20 pennies.

Alex Caby was found dead of starvation, a misadventure, as were the drowning deaths of John and Richard, who were drawing water from a well with a bucket when the rope snapped and they fell in. The sheriff was ordered to declare the value of the bucket.

Cecily was accused of giving a poisoned drink to her husband. Willing herself on the mercy of the court, she was tried before thirty-six men in the churchyard and acquitted, in perpetuity. Andrew was prescribed pills by his doctors and looked after by his valet, Richard. Both swallowed such a quantity of pills that they died soon after. One of the doctors was arrested but acquitted after trial.

The Scarlet Letter

Savage colonial American laws, often influenced by the Puritans, are recounted in a 1624 letter from Virginia colonists to authorities in England, which describe "tyranny-call Lawes written in blood":

> *undeserved death . . . by starveinge, hangeinge, burneinhge, breakinge upon the wheel. . . . Some for stealinge to satisfy their hunger were hanged, and one chained to a tree until he starved to death . . . continual whippings, extraordinary punishments, workage as slaves in irons*

for terms of years (and that for petty offenses) [offenders]
were dayly executed.

Virginia ministers were required to read a set of statutes, the "Articles, Laws and Orders," to the congregation
every Sunday, and failure to attend church was punishable
by loss of a day's food, with a second offense warranting
the whip, and a third offense earning six months of rowing
in the galleys. A person at ordinaries or otherwise not
properly observing the Sabbath paid a 10-shilling fine or
was whipped, and if one acted too proudly and with a high
hand, he was subject to harsher punishment.

Interrupting a minister during services brought the
wiseguy a 20-shilling fine or a four-hour trip to the stocks,
where more pious citizens could hurl garbage at him. A
person was not to ride violently to a sermon or show off a
new colt. A Maine man was fined for unseemly walking,
despite his claim that he ran to save a man from drowning.
Roger Scott was sentenced to be whipped for sleeping late
instead of attending services and for striking the person
who woke him from his godless slumber, while Phillip
Ratcliffe, who spoke against the church, was whipped,
banished, and had his ears cut off.

Death came to those who idolized, blasphemed, or bug-
gered. Cursing one's parents warranted death, unless the
parents were unchristianly negligent or cruel, and a stubborn son who did not hearken to his father's commands
was subject to death, although it was not mandatory.

Ravishing a maid could warrant execution, and adulterers got the whip, but not to exceed forty lashes. For
repeaters, the letter *A* was cut out of cloth and sewed to
their uppermost garments on their arms or back, and they

got a whipping if seen in public without the letter. Captain Kemble kissed his wife in public after three years at sea and spent several hours in the stocks.

Burglars were branded on the right hand with the letter *B* for a first offense and on the other hand and whipped for a second, but if the crime was committed on the Lord's Day, the brand was applied to the forehead. Forgery brought an *F* to the forehand, and a public official who defaced records earned a burn to the face. Gamesters who gambled paid a 10-shilling fine, and one who vexed his adversary in court by pretending great damages paid 40. Lying brought a fine: Ralph Smith paid 20 shillings when he said he saw a whale.

With all the sinning, constables were instructed to keep a close eye on unprofitable fowlers, tobacco takers, and common coasters as well as brawlers, chiders, unruly paupers, and women of light carriage.

Pleas at Wapentake of Aswardhurn (1200s): Thomas claimed that Alan assaulted him on the highway and dragged him into Alan's house. His cape was taken, his arm was broken, and he had one testicle cut off by Alan's wife, Eimma; Ralph cut off the other. The king's sergeant testified that upon investigation he couldn't find the cape but did find two testicles in a cup.

When in Rome . . .

Under the Roman laws of 200–500 CE, if a man accused his wife of adultery, she deserved death but would be placed in a monastery for two years with her head shaved (Constantine), but a woman had no right to accuse a man of the same (Severus). A woman convicted of having sex with her slave was killed, and the "rascally" slave would perish by fire (Constantine).

If a husband served formal written notice three times upon a man whom he suspected of being with his wife and then surprised the two, he could kill him (Constantine). But when a man's wife was pregnant and love was sought but did not appear and the sexual act assumed an unnatural form, the avenging sword would be visited upon the guilty (Constantine). Ravishers of virgins, widows, and nuns were killed since chastity cannot be restored; if the ravisher escaped, he would be hunted down to the farthest reaches of Egypt, Illyria, and Africa (Justinian). Sons or daughters who killed their parents, or vice versa, were to be put to death not by the sword or by fire but rather by being sewed up in a sack with a dog, a cock, a viper, and a monkey, and thrown into the nearest sea or river (Constantine).

A master could kill a slave by striking him with rods or straps, as long as it was accidental, but would be presumed guilty if he killed the slave by hurling him from a precipice, giving him poison, lacerating his body with iron hooks, or burning his limbs with fire (Constantine). And if a master plotted to kill his or her spouse, all of the slaves were to be tortured, even those not involved (Gratian); husbands were encouraged, in "the spirit of the law," to torture innocent slaves to get the details of their wives' infidelities (Alexander).

Obedience to the gods was key to Roman citizenship, and heretic haruspices who predicted the future by inspecting sheep and chicken entrails would be burned (Constantine). Those who consulted with them, or with Chaldeans or magicians, were to be laid low (Constantius).

A person's good name was valued, and whoever discovered a defamatory writing in a house without knowing who placed it there had to immediately tear it up or burn it before it was found, and if he showed it to others he was as liable as its author to be put to death (Valentinian and Valens).

One was prohibited from decorating the saddle of a horse with pearls or emeralds, subject to pentalty of fifty pounds of gold (Justinian). Dealers in hogs were forever exempted from civil service duties (Valentinian). Sturdy beggars would become the slave of those who called them out as frauds, and all members of that uncertain trade would be examined to see if they were really physically infirm or elderly or just idle (Gratian).

People owning land traversed by aqueducts were obliged to plant trees every fifteen feet on both sides, but if the roots began damaging the aqueduct, the trees would have to be cut down (Constantine). Those buying endangered cypress trees on the cypress tree black market would be fined five pounds of gold (Arcadius), and a person improperly seizing land within twelve cubits of the Nile was burned along its banks (Honorius).

But anyone was allowed to kill a lion (Honorius), and the May Festival was reestablished, although, by necessity, subject to strictures of modesty, decency, and chastity (Arcadius).

A Remembrance of the Plague

The Remembrancia, a cache of letters found in the Town Clerk's Record Room in London, records some of the many laws written to combat the spread of the plague, which waxed and waned between 1347 and 1665.

In 1580, to preserve the city from drawing God's wrath, citizens were prohibited from frequenting infamous houses and unchaste plays, and strangers and artificers and those of no church were to be prevented from pestering more pious citizens.

In 1581, Rowland Winter and his family were visited by the plague. Although skilled in cutting leather and making jerkins and having provided Her Majesty with the service of his art, Winter was restrained from going out of his house.

In 1582, laws regulated burial at St. Paul's churchyard, where so many bodies had piled up on one another that the corpses were being laid open. In September the number of dead greatly increased, partly due to lax enforcement of street cleaning rules. Citizens with any signs of disease were prevented from attending the Firdeswide Fair, and all those wishing to go had to obtain a certificate. A survey was commissioned to count all infected inns and victual houses that had tabled customers in the previous two months, but the result was misliked because the tally was too long. A scaffold collapsed at Paris Gardens, killing many; like the plague itself, the tragedy was attributable to the hand of God, since the amusement was being held on the Sabbath day.

In 1583, the numbers of infected had much increased,

and orders were issued barring the assembly of people to see plays, bearbaiting, fencing, and other great spectacles to which the worst sort of people resorted.

In 1606, an order was passed requiring each infected house to be guarded by two watchmen, to prevent occupants from leaving, and marshals were appointed to keep beggars out of the city.

In 1625, as per *The Bills of Mortality*, 35,403 London citizens died of the plague.

In 1629, all streets were ordered to be kept swept and clean, and in 1630 each infected house, with guards posted, had to have a red cross or a "Lord, Have Mercy Upon Us" sign posted on the door. The son of butcher John Thomas had plague sores, also known as plague tokens or buboes, and then died, and the entire family was sent to the pesthouse. All assemblies for the continuance of acquaintance, including stage plays, tumbling, and rope dancing, were to be suppressed, and people who died were to be buried late at night, so their relatives wouldn't linger and themselves become infected.

In 1636, it was found that the red cross and "Lord, Have Mercy Upon Us" signs were being deliberately placed in obscure places so they could barely be seen, and that few infected houses had watchmen. Officers were directed to strictly enforce the law, and those who failed in their duties were sent to Newgate prison as an example. Anxiety was expressed over streets pestered with beggars, rogues, wanderers, and dissolute persons, many with plague sores about them.

By September 1655, the plague was killing seven thousand Londoners a week, and desperate officials killed upward of forty thousand dogs and twenty to eighty thousand cats. Daniel Defoe, in his fictional but historically accurate *Journal of the Plague Year*, reports that eighteen to twenty watchmen were killed by occupants of plague houses seeking to escape.

Miraculously, just a month or two later, the disease began to burn itself out, never to return.

Those Jews

Under Spain's *Las Siete Partidas* ("The Seven Part Code"), first compiled during the reign of Alfonso X the Wise (circa 1265) and put into effect decades later, Jews were tolerated, barely, and their rights reluctantly protected.

Jews *were* considered fit to live among other people (Title XXIV), but it was always on the minds of men that Jews descended from those who crucified the Lord Jesus Christ (Law I).

Jews were to be left alone, although those accused of celebrating Good Friday by stealing children and fastening them to crosses and making images of wax and crucifying them were to be brought before the king and put to death if they were guilty, no matter how many of them there were. And for their own safety, Jews were prohibited from going out on Good Friday; if they did, they did so at their own risk (Law II).

Because of past perfidies and because they disowned Jesus by shamefully putting Him to death on the Cross, Jews were not allowed to hold the honors and privileges of office, where they might oppress a Christian (Law III).

Jews were not allowed to erect new synagogues or to

paint them or build to a greater height than existing ones, but Christians were prohibited from defacing them, loitering nearby, stealing from them, or putting animals in them (Law IV). No judge or court could serve or summon or otherwise disrupt Jews on their Sabbath day (Law V).

No compulsion could be used to try to forcibly convert Jews, but Christians could try with kind words, and if they were successful, any Jew who stoned or killed the new convert would be burned himself (Law VI). Any Christian so unfortunate as to convert to Judaism would meet with death (Law VII).

Jews and Christians were prohibited from eating or drinking together, and no Jews would dare bathe in the company of Christians (Law VIII). Only Jews of great boldness and insolence would sleep with Christian women, and they would be put to death, especially since Christian women were "the wives of our Lord" (Law IX).

To protect the Jews, it was necessary that Jews bear some distinguishing mark upon their heads, men and women alike, and any Jew who didn't bear such a mark would pay 10 maravedis of gold and, if he couldn't afford it, would receive ten lashes (Law XI)—for his own good.

A similar fate befell Christians living in Muslim countries of the Middle East from the seventh century on, who had to submit to the Pact of Umar or be hunted down as enemies and rebels. "In the name of God, the Merciful," Christians (and Jews, and others) were granted protection as long as they agreed to the pact, which was a short list of rules governing worship and daily behavior.

Church bells had to ring softly and services could not be recited loudly in the presence of a Muslim. Loud chanting was not allowed at a funeral. Gates were to be opened wide to Muslim travelers, who had to be given food and lodging for three days, and when Muslims wished to take their seats at an assembly, Christians had to rise up in deference.

Muslims were not to be imitated through the wearing of similar clothes or the parting of the hair, and Christians had to wear leather or cord girdles around their waists, not cloth or silk, and had to shave their heads in front.

The Law Code of Gortyn (Crete, 450 BCE): Raping a free woman cost a freeman 100 staters and raping a serf, 5 drachmas. Debauching a house slave by force cost 2 staters, but if she had been debauched before in the daytime only 1 obol, and if at night, 2 obols.

Genghis

The softer side of Genghis Khan is revealed by his little-known love for the law and its administration.

Khan's Great Yasa is said to have been written on rolls of parchment and hidden from all but Khan and his closest advisers, and no part of the scrolls has ever been found. But detailed accounts were recorded by historians of the day, and most scholars agree that the laws did exist, either as a unified text or more likely as a series of individual laws stitched together at the peak of Khan's rule in the early 1300s.

Under the Yasa all religions were to be respected, "thy neighbor was to be loved as thyself," and old people and beggars were to be treated kindly. No titles or honorifics were to be used; even the Khan himself was to be called by his regular name.

Spies and sorcerers were put to death, along with those who urinated into the water or choked on food, with capital criminals possibly being buried under a heavy layer of plush carpeting. But a murderer could ransom himself by paying a fine: 40 golden coins for a Mohammedan, 1 donkey for a Chinese.

Food and hospitality were to be given to passing wayfarers, and tax breaks were available to the devout. A hunter who allowed an animal to escape during a community hunt was to be beaten with a stick.

A man could get drunk three times in a month, but a soldier who didn't return the pack dropped by the warrior in front of him during battle was executed. A man in whose possession a stolen horse was found was to return it along with nine new ones, but if he was unable to do so, his children would be taken instead; if he had no children, he himself would be slaughtered like a sheep.

One couldn't wash clothes until they were completely worn out, and food eaten in the presence of another had to be shared. A person couldn't eat food offered by another until the offering person tasted it first, and one couldn't eat more than his comrades, or step over a fire on which food was being cooked. A person couldn't dip his hands in water, and when an animal was to be eaten, its feet had to be tied, its belly ripped open, and its heart squeezed in the hand until the animal died.

The Roman Ecloga (800s): A person convicted of perjury had his or her tongue cut out.

Precise People

As a rebuke to Puritans and "precise people" trying to enforce strict observance of the Sabbath, in 1633 King Charles issued the Declaration of Sports, an unusual law promoting fun and games:

> [W]ith our own ears, we heard the general complaint of our people, that they were barred from all lawful recreation and exercise upon the Sunday's afternoon . . . which cannot but breed a great discontentment. . . . [O]ur pleasure likewise is that . . . our good people be not disturbed, letted or discouraged from any lawful recreation such as dancing . . . archery . . . , leaping, vaulting . . . May-games, Whitsum-ales, and Morris dances: and the setting of May-poles.

The law did instruct citizens to attend Sunday morning services before letting loose and continued a ban on bear-baiting and bowling. But to stick it to the precise people, the statute required that ministers read the law about fun and games from the pulpit every Sunday.

The Bloody Code

English criminal statutes of the 1700s ("The Bloody Code") mandated death for the most trivial of crimes.

Sixteen-year-old James Belbin was accused of breaking

into the house of neighboring widow Sarah Gosling, whom he knew well. According to the indictment, he stole a silk petticoat, breeches, gowns, coats, and a flounced stuff ditto.

Ms. Gosling testified that she found her window open and traced a trail of silk bits and footprints in the snow leading to the street, and then found two of her gowns in Mr. Cooper's pawnshop, and that all she wanted was her gowns back. Mr. Gardner, clerk of the pawnshop, testified that Belbin had sold the gowns to him, claiming he bought them from a Ms. Hambro. Ms. Hambro testified she knew nothing about any gowns. Belbin testified that he just happened to see two gowns dropped in the street and then pawned them.

A jury quickly found Belbin guilty, and the court sentenced him to death. But the same jury humbly recommended him to mercy, and, as was often the case, the judge accepted the recommendation without objection. The boy's life was spared.

The Spanking Machine

In his *The Rationale of Punishment*, the eminent utilitarian philosopher Jeremy Bentham (1748–1832) proposed a spanking machine:

> *Of all these different modes of punishment, whipping is the most frequently in use . . . the quantity of force to be employed in its application is altogether entrusted to the caprice of the executioner. He may make the punishment as trifling or as severe as he pleases. . . .*

The following contrivance would, in a measure, obviate this inconvenience: A machine might be made, which should put in motion certain elastic rods of cane or whalebone, the number and size of which might be determined by the law . . . when there were many delinquents to be punished, his [the official's] time might be saved, and the terror of the scene heightened . . . by increasing the number of the machines, and subjecting all the offenders to punishment at the same time.

Cattle Call

At a hearing at the Courthouse in Plymouth, Massachusetts, on May 22, 1627, known as the Plymouth Colony Division of Cattle, livestock acquired from various ships were divided into twelve lots, with each lot given to a group of thirteen Pilgrims.

In addition to two she-goats, the lots consisted of:

1. *The least of four Black heifers.*

2. *The Great Black Cow, and the lesser of two steers.*

3. *The Red Cow and her calf.*

4. *One of four heifers.*

5. *The Blind heifer.*

6. *The lesser of the Black Cows and the biggest of two steers.*

7. *A Black calf, and a calf to come out of the Black Cow.*

8. The Red Heifer.

9. The Smooth-Horned heifer.

10. The White heifer.

11. The heifer from the Great White Back Cow.

12. The Great White Back Cow.

So Yesterday

I base my fashion sense on what doesn't itch.

—Gilda Radner

Regimes have often restricted the clothing their citizens may wear, with the Greeks and Romans expressing a particular concern over trousers and slacks.

Greek historian Herodotus, known as the Father of Western History, was appalled at the barbarians' failure to mix and match, noting the men who "wear leathern trousers, and have all their other garments of leather" (*The Histories*, 1.71.2–4, 5.49.3–4). Herodotus also turned his keen eye on the prissy Persian guys—their well-turned-out warriors "glittered with gold," wore the tiara, and draped their lithe bodies with elegant sleeved tunics (*The Histories*, 7.61.1).

Cicero, Roman orator and philosopher, lamented the non-designer knockoffs that were flooding the border of the empire. "I am marvelously fond of . . . our native brand most of all. . . . [I]t is now . . . the trousered tribes from over the Alps . . . so overwhelmed that no trace of the old gay charm is any more to be found" (*Letters to His Friends*, 9.15).

Strict statutes soon followed, with the Codex Theodosianus 14.10.2–3 (433 CE) banning trousers outright; fashion victims caught by crisply uniformed Praetorian guards were, perhaps justifiably, expelled from the empire. Trampy boots were also banned under the codex, and later silk ensembles.

In 1574, Queen Elizabeth I became so concerned with her kingdom's obsession with sartorial extravagance that she feared "the manifest decay of the whole realm . . . the wasting and undoing of a great number of young gentlemen . . . who allured by the vain showing of those things . . . run into debts and shifts."

The queen signed the Statute of Apparel (1574), which prohibited both men and women from wearing, among other things, silk of the color purple, leopard, rapiers, netherstocks, foins, pantofles of velvet, skeans, grosgrain, and kirtles.

Fear of revolution and plaid prompted England's Dress Act of 1746, part of the Act of Proscription of the same year. The Dress Act, designed to crush Scottish cultural autonomy, banned the wearing of kilts and tartans, on pain of seven years' service on a foreign plantation. The act was repealed in 1782 with the Repeal of the Act Prescribing the Wearing of Highland Dress:

> *Listen Men. . . . The King and Parliament of Britain have Forever abolished the act against the Highland Dress. . . . This must bring great joy to every Highland heart. You are no longer bound down to the unmanly dress of the Lowlander.*

2

In the Neighborhood

Sometimes the strangest things in life can be found just around the corner, and the statutes governing where we live are no exception. Our most respectable states have laws governing electric eels, walking catfish, and foreign fats, and our all-American towns have statutes barring us from breaking into dog pounds and from building an atom bomb. Here's a collection of laws from the counties, states, and cities in which we live—we must promise to do our best to avoid breaking them.

New Hampshire

New Hampshire's overbearing laws belie its "Live Free or Die" motto.

Under New Hampshire law, "no person shall perform

any work or play on the Lord's Day except works of necessity and mercy," though the Lord apparently smiles on dog racing and gambling thereon, which are exempt from the law (Sunday Business Activities, § 332-D:1–3). And the Lord's name apparently can be taken in vain because another law allows individual towns to disregard the preceding statute and do as they please on Sundays (§ 332-D:4). For example, it is perfectly legal to watch a movie on Sunday in Concord, as long as the movie starts after 2:00 p.m. (Morals and Conduct, Ch. 14, Art. 14-1–3).

A rock formation shaped like a person's profile, the Old Man of the Mountain, is the state's official emblem, although it collapsed into a heap of rubble in 2003 (State Emblems, § 3:1). There are ten different state songs (§ 3:7), none you've ever heard of.

In New Hampshire, no showman, tumbler, rope dancer, or ventriloquist "shall charge to exhibit feats of agility or horsemanship or sleight of hand without a license" (Shows and Open Air Meetings, § 286:1), and lightning rod salesmen must be licensed (Occupations and Professions, § 323:1). Standard-size produce boxes must contain exactly 2,162.89 cubic inches (Farm Produce, § 434:1), and the size of apples must be determined "by taking the transverse diameter of the smallest fruit in the package at right angles to the stem and blossom ends" (Apples, § 434:21).

Ice dealers who don't weigh the ice on request are subject to a $50 fine (Ice, § 434:7), and others who deliver ice from a wagon and refuse to weigh it receive a violation (§ 434:8). Spite fences—erected for the purpose of annoying a neighbor—cannot exceed five feet (Spite Fences, Ch. 476:1).

New Hampshire's wilderness laws are equally stern. Hunters, except those hunting waterfowl, should wear hunter orange with a dominant wavelength between 595 and 605 nanometers and an excitation purity of not less than 85 percent (Fish and Game, § 207:38-b). It is forbidden to shoot wildlife that has been chased up a tree by a dog, unless the owner of the dog or someone in his hunting party is present, in which case shooting the helpless animal is perfectly okay (Dogs, § 207:13-b). A prohibition against shooting human beings has been repealed (Fish and Game, § 207.37).

No person obviously on his way from or to hunting can have a ferret in his possession (Fish and Game, § 207:6), and one can't destroy a muskrat house (§ 210:4). A person cannot introduce a wolf into New Hampshire (§ 207:61).

Those who really must may drive their vehicles over frozen lakes, but can't drive more than thirty-five miles per hour after dark on Back Lake in Pittsburg (Fish and Game, § 215-A:4-a). One who chooses to dig a hole into a frozen lake instead of driving atop it must mark the hole with a stake if the hole is more than 112 square inches in area and left unattended, unless the hole is covered with a bob house (§ 211:17-c).

If the executive director for distribution entrusts to a person's care any fish or fry, under no circumstances can that person buy, sell, or offer them for sale or put them in private waters or carry them beyond the limits of the state (Fish and Game, § 211:14). Only suckers can be used for fertilizer (§ 211:15).

Grand Guignol

In the city of Grand Forks, North Dakota, pursuant to City Code Article 1, it is illegal to:

- Assault a police dog (§ 9-0106).
- Throw a snowball upon public or private property (§ 9-0123).
- Fail to confine a dog or cat in heat (§ 11-0113).
- Counterfeit cat and dog tags (§ 11-0119).
- Throw candy from a float during a parade (§ 9-0211).
- Break into a dog pound (§ 11-0118).

Maine

The Marine Worm Tax has been repealed! (Maine Revised Statutes (Title 36)).

Fortunately, the Marine Worm Fund (Title 12 (1977)), not to be confused with the medieval Concordat of Worms (1122), a treaty between the pope and the ancient Romans, is still going strong, since, by law, "The Marine Worm Fund shall not lapse" (subsection 3).

The Quahog Tax (Title 12) and the Sea Moss License (Title 2) have also been repealed, but old school still applies to sea cucumbers, which require a drag license and can't be taken if they're over five foot six inches in width, on penalty of not less than $100 (Title 12 (2005)).

As of 2003, do not try to sell lead sinkers containing lead, since "A person may not sell a lead sinker [of under half an ounce] for fishing that contains any lead," or pay a fine of between $100 and $500 (§ 12663-A).

More provocative are 1993 laws prohibiting sea urchins and lobsters from being together aboard boats (Title 12), and 1977's shameful Green Crab Fencing Program, designed to segregate green crabs from soft-shell clams (Title 12).

Move It!

In Alabama, a voter spending more than four minutes in the voting booth can be asked if he or she needs help. If not, and the polling place is crowded, the voter is given one more minute to vote and then asked to leave (Code of Alabama, § 17-9-13(b) (2006)).

Deadwood

Pretend cowboy town Deadwood, South Dakota, former home of Wild Bill Hickock and Calamity Jane, is according to its chamber of commerce, still known for its wild ways and an "ideal place to release your inner outlaw." Local sheriffs keep the peace with laws tough as nails and plenty of them, and with both an assault *and* a burglary on the books in 2007, Deadwood tinhorns are cracking the whip on a lawless posse of out-of-town gringos who could, at least theoretically, drink, fight, gamble, and cat around with loose women.

For those wild parties where "the fun doesn't end when the sun goes down," it is illegal to mix one drink with another without a permit (Deadwood Ordinances, Ch. 9.08.010) and to carry an unconcealed slingshot, sandbag, dagger, dirk knife, slapjack, or brass knuckles (Ch. 9.24.010). Gunslingers shooting a revolver earlier than ten minutes before the theater opens or a skit begins could be strung up, or at least be issued a violation (Ch. 9.24.020).

You'll be run out of town if you try to use slugs (Ch. 9.16.040) or engage in psychic powers, spirits, seership, palmistry, necromancy, science cards, charms, potions, magnetism, or Oriental mysteries (5.52.010). Of course, it is unlawful to keep a house of ill fame (Ch. 9.08.020).

For the decent folk of the town, imperfect plumbing is outlawed (Ch. 8.16.020(A)), as is discharging slop, beer washings, and offal into drains, spouts, or public places (Ch. 8.16.020(B)(2)), and even locals playing bingo for charity must defer to visiting gamblers and their wallets by using separate entrances and exits (Ch. 5.08.010(C)). But moving a building along the street is allowed, with a permit (Ch. 15.28.010).

Rough justice prevails when it comes to Deadwood's signs. Those with revolving or rotating parts or moved by the wind or breeze are prohibited, as are signs that present even an illusion of motion (Ch. 15.32.130.6), and no sign shall ever flash, move, rotate, blink, flicker, pulse, or even scintillate (Ch. 15.32.130.7). In general, no sign shall project images or sound designed to attract attention (Ch. 15.32.060.12). Furthermore, in rough-and-tumble Deadwood, none of the town's twenty-nine casinos can hang a sign that contains the word *casino* (Ch. 15.32.130.23).

Keep the Change

In Canada, a person doesn't have to accept more than twenty-five pennies (Currency Act, § 8 (2) § 10).

Rhode Island

Our smallest state leaves a big legal footprint.

"No person shall possess the meats of more than six (6) shellfish while shellfishing" (Rhode Island General Laws, Shellfish, § 20-6-21), and woe to those who wrap what they catch in secondhand paper (Food and Beverages, § 11-16-3). "Poisoning in general" is discouraged (§ 11-16-6), but poisoning with intent to kill carries a life sentence (§ 11-16-5), and one who cuts or bites off the limb or member of another gets between one and twenty years (Mayhem, § 11-29-1), but only if the conduct is intentional.

Idealist islanders still tilt at windmills, since any person who erects one within twenty-five rods of a road is subject to a fine (Highway Law, § 11-22-6). Stealing stone walls is considered a heavy crime and punishable as larceny (Theft of Historic Stone Walls, § 11-41-32).

Those on either end of "Theft of Poultry—Receiving Stolen Poultry" (§ 11-41-9) can get a year in jail—it's only fair—and shopping carts, egg baskets, and bakery and poultry boxes are registered with the secretary of state (Grocery and Laundry Carts, Milk Cases, Egg Baskets, and Bakery Containers, § 11-41.1-2), and possession of same by unauthorized personnel is deemed larceny (§ 11-41.1-4). Of course, removal of items from these containers in the supermarket parking lot is prohibited § (11-41.1-6).

Trust in the marketplace ensures continued prosperity for all, thus the urgent need for public weighers (Public Weighers, § 47-7-1) and for stiff penalties for impersonating the town sealer, auctioneer, corder, or fence viewer (§ 11-14-2). The Cat Identification Program (§ 4-22-3) further safeguards against fraud and assorted flimflammery.

Smile, Dammit!

In 1948, Pocatello, Illinois, passed a statute: "It is prohibited for pedestrians and motorists to display frowns, grimaces, scowls, threatening and glowering looks, gloomy and depressed facial appearances, generally all of which reflect unfavorably upon the city's reputation." The law was repealed, but SmileFest is still held every September.

South Carolina

South Carolina is justifiably careful of its protected wildlife and scenic shoreline and has laws to match.

Wild turkey feathers may be used in painting and sculpture but only with official identification and permission from the Indian Arts and Craft Board Act (Title 50, § 50). This law in no way authorizes the sale of turkey capes, beards, and fans (§ 50).

It is unlawful to impale fish on hooks by snagging or jerking within one thousand feet downstream of a hydro-electric dam (Title 50, Ch. 13, § 50-13-12). Eel pots, bows and arrows, gigs, and spears may be used to take non-game fish (§ 50-213-1115), but dynamite is not allowed (§ 50-13-1440).

The daily creel limit is forty (§ 50-13-210), and no more than one fish caught can be an Arkansas blue catfish over thirty-six inches, at least in Lakes Marion and Moultre (§ 50-13-390). It is illegal to own or sell an electric eel or walking catfish (§ 50-13-1630) or wild live rock (§ 50-5-2305). Legally acceptable bait includes soap, dough balls, meat, grapes, and fish cut into at least three parts (§ 50-13-1187-A). On both the Big Pee Dee and the Little Pee Dee rivers, live fish and bream can be used (§ 50-213-1115).

Using yoyos to fish is prohibited (§ 50-13-1190).

Get It Right

In Joliet, Illinois, be careful what you say and especially how you say it:

> *The only official, correct and proper pronunciation of the name of this city shall be Jo-li-et: the accent on the first syllable, with the "o" in the first syllable pronounced in its long sound, as in the words "so", "no" and "foe" and any other pronunciations to be discouraged as interfering with the desired uniformity in respect to the proper pronunciation of the name of this city (Code of Ordinances of City of Joliet, Ch. 2, Art. 1, § 2-8).*

Sink Like a Stone

Bales of cocaine, not captains, go down with the ship on narco-submarines, allowing their commanders to swim free from prosecution when apprehended on the high seas. The Drug Trafficking Vessel Interdiction Act of 2008 is now closing this drug dealer escape hatch.

The act was passed to torpedo the use of semisubmersible submarines that sink to the bottom on command, taking the evidence with them. Barely visible from above, the subs carry several tons of cocaine and have a hidden scuttling mechanism. When the boat is intercepted, sailors jump into the water, knowing they'll be rescued by their pursuers and then quickly released for want of evidence.

Now, the sailors can be put away for twenty years merely if the vessel is not legally registered, and the law also allows U.S. agents to make arrests in international waters.

Attorney P. Federico Bower was perturbed when his supposedly pleasure-boating client was arrested just because he happened to be aboard a self-sinking sub that coincidentally went down when it was hailed by drug enforcement officers. He points out that no drugs were retrieved, but now it doesn't really matter.

Stormy Weather

Whoever issues or publishes a fake weather report and claims it's from the Weather Bureau is subject to imprisonment for not more than ninety days (18 U.S.C. § 2074).

Vermont

Citizens of scenic Vermont value their peace and quiet, and a person convicted of common barratry will be fined not more than $50 (Barratry, § 701); touting is also subject to a $500 fine or one year imprisonment or both (Touting Prohibited, § 2156).

The word *mapley* or words of similar import shall not appear on labels or containers of syrup products that are merely maple flavored as opposed to the real thing (Maple Products, Ch. 32), and branding an animal costs $3 per brand (Brands, § 3072).

Urine Farms, Chapter 69, was repealed in 1989, but Foreign Fats are still prohibited (Foreign Fats Prohibited, Ch. 153).

England's Dumbest Laws

England's UKTV channel presented to nearly four thousand people a list of what it claimed were the most bizarre laws in all of Britain and asked them to choose the dumbest and most ridiculous (percent of votes in parentheses):

- It is illegal to die in the Houses of Parliament (27 percent).
- It is an act of treason to place a postage stamp bearing the British monarch upside down (7 percent).
- In Liverpool, it is illegal for a woman to be topless except as a clerk in a tropical fish store (6 percent).

- Mince pies cannot be eaten on Christmas Day (5 percent).
- In Scotland, if someone knocks on the door and requires the use of your toilet, you must let him or her enter (4 percent).
- A pregnant woman can legally relieve herself anywhere she wants, including in a policeman's helmet (4 percent).
- The head of any dead whale found on the British coast automatically becomes the property of the king, and the tail, of the queen (3.5 percent).
- It is illegal to avoid telling the tax man anything you do not want him to know, but legal not to tell him information you do not mind him knowing (3 percent).
- It is illegal to enter the Houses of Parliament in a suit of armor (3 percent).
- In the city of York, it is legal to murder a Scotsman within the ancient city walls, but only if he is carrying a bow and arrow (2 percent).

Nearly half of those surveyed admitted to breaking the law by eating mince pies on Christmas Day.

Slacking Off

In Alabama, a person who deliberately injures himself to get out of performing a legal duty or to excite sympathy or obtain alms or charitable relief is guilty of a felony (Code of Alabama, § 13A-14-1).

(Get) Down with the Ship

In Canada, anyone who prevents or interferes with the rescuing of a stranded ship or vessel in distress, or passengers aboard same, faces five years in prison. Impeding the salvaging of a shipwreck is also a punishable crime (R.S., c. C-34, s. 438).

Massachusetts

"It's All Here," the state slogan of Massachusetts, surely applies to its statute books, which contain just about everything, whether sensible or not.

Selling a stink bomb is a crime (Crimes Against Public Peace, § 269(15), and anyone using a boom box without earphones in public can be jailed for a month (Crimes Against the Person, § 265-42).

Entering or riding a horse that's painted in order to win a race gets six months in jail (Crimes Against Public Policy, § 271-32), as does taking an exam in the place of another or selling a term paper so someone else can grab the academic credit (§ 271-50).

It's a crime against chastity, morality, decency, and good order to interrupt a funeral procession by fast driving (Crimes Against Chastity, Morality, Decency and Good Order, § 272-42), as is making too much noise in a library (§ 272-41) and owning a restaurant with a booth that has curtains, preventing other diners from seeing in (§ 272-25).

Selling candy laced with arsenic is punishable by a steep fine of $50 to $100 (Crimes Against Public Health, § 270-10).

Gesundheit

In Manteno, Illinois, "No person shall drop, throw or place any used facial tissue or paper handkerchief upon any public way" (Manteno Village Code, Title 5, Ch. 1, § 5-1-11).

Peace in Our Time

The city council of Chino, California, has had enough and declared the city a nuclear-free zone. Along with bans on graffiti, disorderly conduct, and parking near fire hydrants, Chino has determined that nuclear war is a danger to the health and safety of its citizens and "totally unacceptable." It has barred the production, maintenance, and storage of nuclear devices. Nuclear testing within city limits is also prohibited (Chino Municipal Code, Division IX, Ch. 9.60 (2000)).

Long May It Wave

In West Virginia, it is a "crime against the government" to display or possess a red or black flag (West Virginia Code, § 61-1.6).

Utah

Utah lowers the boom on its wild residents and their libertine lifestyles.

Utah residents can't use corn or hominy as fishing bait or even a salamander, although mottled sculpin, redside shiner, and speckled dace are allowed (Utah Administrative Code, Bait, R657-13-12), as long as they are not used to catch gizzard shad, virgin spinedance, or least chub, all of which are off-limits (Prohibited Fish, R657-30). Dipnets may not be used as a primary means to catch fish, except when catching Bonneville cisco in Bear Lake (R657-13-10).

As of May 2009, only the Division of Water Resources can engage in cloud seeding, the dispersal of silver iodide or dry ice into clouds to make them rain (Cloud Seeding, R653-5-2(1)), and those seeking to modify the weather need a permit to do so (R653-5-5), although a permit is not required for one merely wishing to suppress fog (R653-5-5). In Salt Lake County, catteries *are* permitted to keep dogs (Animals, 8.03.40), but those wishing to keep a feral cat colony need proof that the cats have been ear tipped (8.03.140). It is unlawful to possess an unleashed dog on even-numbered days in Millcreek Canyon (8.04.170).

In the big city, a person can't sell swill milk (Salt Lake City Municipal Code, Food Regulations, 8.20.010), but in Salt Lake County, duck, turkey, guinea, and geese eggs may be sold as long as they are kept separate from chicken eggs and are of good quality when used in cream pies, French pastries, meringue, salad dressing, and hollandaise sauce (Food and Beverage Control, 6.24.170). An official milkman can have only occasional and casual contact with his customers (6.40.010).

Given Salt Lake County's well-known wild streak, there is an 11:00 p.m. curfew for sixteen-year-olds (Salt Lake County Municipal Code, 10.60.0-030), and police can arrest for riot a mob of two or more people who engage in alarming or tumultuous behavior or who are even thinking about doing so in the future (Riot, 11.12.010).

An adult may not display or distribute sex paraphernalia or devices to a minor (Distribution of Sex Paraphernalia to Minors (9.20.010), unless that minor is one's child, in which case distribution or display is perfectly legal (9.20.010(D)), though this sort of behavior is certainly not encouraged.

Silent Night

In Little Rock, Arkansas, it is illegal to honk your horn after 9:00 p.m. at any place where sandwiches or cold drinks are served (Little Rock, Arkansas Municipal Code, § 18-53, Art. II, § 18-54).

The Father of All Turkmen

Turkmenbashi, Glorious Father of All Turkmen and president for life, was not a humble man. Leader of the former Soviet Republic of Turkmenistan beginning in 1990, the dictator (real name: Saparmurat Niyazov) instituted a series of laws and decrees that would have made Stalin blush.

Turkmenbashi renamed the months of the calendar after himself and his family; January was Turkmenbashi, and April was called Gurbansoltan, after his mother, who died in 1948. Clock and watch faces displayed his portrait and prospective drivers had to memorize his spiritual guides before earning their licenses. In 2003, Turkmenbashi was the winner of the Magtymguly International Prize for poetry, awarded by himself.

In 2005, it was declared that doctors were to no longer take the Hippocratic Oath but rather swear sole allegiance to Turkmenbashi; in 1998, worshipful government scientists named a 670-pound meteorite in his honor.

Turkmenbashi's 2004 decree that an ice palace holding one thousand visitors be built in the Kara-Kum desert, central Asia's hottest region, was never carried out, but his laws of the same year banning long hair and beards on men, and especially the hated goatee, were strictly implemented, as was a 2003 dictum that young schoolgirls wear braids. Turkmenbashi also forbade one from listening to car radios, and banned opera and ballet performances, since they were unnecessary.

During a critical speech in April 2004, the Leader of All Ethnic Turkmen banned teeth caps made of gold, observing that dogs with healthy teeth were given bones to gnaw, and that "those of you whose teeth have fallen out did not gnaw on bones."

Turkmenbashi naturally left no plans for a successor, and his eccentric laws were repealed after his 2006 death.

3

Strange Things, Strange Places

Most of our laws govern the lives of ordinary people doing ordinary things in familiar places, but unique opportunities arise and new frontiers open, and those representing the establishment struggle to catch up. From the mysteries of the afterlife to the ends of the earth, this chapter concerns the law's grasp over strange people, places, and things.

Black Hole

A collision course is brewing between supercollider particle physicists and frightened citizens concerned with the fate of the world. Jurisdiction over black holes and strangelets is now an issue before the U.S. Court of Appeals, while the European Court of Human Rights decides whether mad scientists risk total obliteration of our beloved planet.

In *Sancho v. U.S. Department of Energy, CERN et al.* (U.S. Ct. Appeals, Ninth Circuit, No. 08-17389), filed in 2008, advocates of life on earth as we know it sued to postpone operation of the Large Hadron Collider, constructed by the European Organization for Nuclear Research (CERN) in Geneva, Switzerland. According to the lawsuit, the sixteen-mile-circumference atom smasher could create novel forms of matter existing nowhere else in the universe except possibly in the interior of a collapsed supernova star, and convert the planet we know and love into either a large lump of "strange matter" or a small black hole. The plaintiffs further contend that collider proponents have admitted that such a scenario is merely "unlikely" or "very unlikely," still too close for comfort for those who support our future existence. Chastened CERN physicists now claim the risk is minuscule to nonexistent, based on their own studies concerning possible doomsday scenarios.

In the United States, an appeal arose after the case was dismissed on purely jurisdictional grounds, with the court finding that U.S. involvement in CERN wasn't sufficient to warrant a ruling on the mostly European project.

In Europe, some scientists claim that a mini black hole could swallow the earth from the inside out in a matter of minutes. Such a result would, the suit claims, violate the legal rights of all people currently alive on the planet. A bid for an injunction was denied but the main lawsuit will be heard soon, barring any tragic accidents.

Tempting Fate

In New Orleans, it is unlawful to engage in the business of fortune-telling, astrology, or palmistry to

> *settle lovers' quarrels . . . locate buried or hidden treasures . . . remove evil influences . . . reveal secrets . . . or to bring together the bitterest enemies converting them into staunchest friends.*

The law continues, "But nothing herein contained shall apply to any branch of medical *science* (New Orleans Municipal Code, § 54-312).

Spellbound

In Everett, Washington, its it unlawful for a hypnotist to exhibit or display a person under his influence in a window or public place outside the theater where the performance is being given, upon pain of six months in jail (Everett Municipal Code, § 9.24.010).

Karma Control

In this life and the next, China is again asserting its heavy hand over Tibet, through the registration and control of reincarnating monks.

In 2007, more than fifty years after "liberating" the Himalayan country, China's State Religious Affairs Bureau Order No. 5 decreed that all Tibetan Buddhist temples file a "Reincarnation Application" on behalf of any monks wishing to migrate to the next world.

These applications must be submitted to various government agencies for approval, and a failure to file the required paperwork, which includes fourteen articles, principles, conditions, and procedures, renders a monk's transcendence "illegal or invalid." According to the Religious Affairs Bureau, the rules are "an important move to institutionalize the management of reincarnation of living Buddhas."

In a land where religious figures are believed to be reincarnated in order to pursue their good works, the 2007 law is an attempt by China to control Tibetan factions competing to appoint a new wave of spiritual leaders, including the next Dalai Lama.

Enter the Dragon

"Tongue splitting" has caught on so fast that legislators everywhere have scrambled to regulate the practice. The lizard look, which splits the tongue from tip to base, is now regulated by statutes in an ever-growing number of states, most of whom require the procedure to be done by a doctor or dentist.

Going to Extremes

The long arm of the law does not extend to our planet's poles.

No one owns the North Pole, although various countries have tried. When in 2000 a pilot abandoned his plane on the ice because of engine trouble, Canada asserted its jurisdiction by charging him with littering. In 2008, Russia dispatched a nuclear-powered icebreaker and two mini subs to stake a claim by planting a titanium-encased flag 13,200 feet below the ocean's frozen surface: aptly named expedition leader Artur Chilingarov coldly declared, "The Arctic is ours."

Things up north sometimes go awry. In 1906, federal charges for murder in the Arctic were brought against Captain Klinkenberger, who was said to have shot to death his chief engineer, poisoned his foremost hand, and left his engineer and a seaman to die on an ice floe; his steward brought charges after having been left to die in Siberia.

Jurisdiction is a problem. In 1926, Eskimo Kudlooktoo confessed to having killed one Professor Marvin, but no court accepted the case. In 1869, Arctic explorer Captain Hall shot and killed a seaman in the Arctic Circle for impromptitude. Lacking a jurisdictional base, authorities tried to bring charges against Hall in Jersey City, New Jersey. The gambit was apparently unsuccessful.

The continent of Antarctica, home of the South Pole, is controlled by the Antarctic Treaty (1961), signed by forty-six countries and consisting of fourteen articles and two hundred more pacts and agreements. But overlapping territorial claims and conflicting jurisdictions ensure what one law review article describes as Wild West law, or no law at all.

At the South Pole a few thousand hard-drinking residents are crowded into bleak "stations," and untoward incidents do occur. The methanol-ingestion death of Australian astrophysicist Rodney Marks in 2000 was widely reported to be the Antarctic's first murder, but no charges were brought after years of police investigation. A sudden evacuation of McMurdo Station residents in 2001 after reports of unexplained injuries and black eyes was apparently the result of a drunken brawl.

The animal kingdom is not exempt from this bipolar crime wave—the Antarctic's gentoo penguins are noted for stealing nest-making stones from each other, and South Pole scientists on Marion Island were shocked as they filmed a male fur seal sexually assaulting a penguin of unknown gender for half an hour.

Human nature knows no bounds. Each year Antarctic residents make an annual ceremony of placing a custom-designed marker at the ever-shifting geographical South Pole, the exact bottom of the world. According to a report from the local newspaper, *The Antarctic Sun*, the historic markers are being stolen and taken as souvenirs.

Crafty Science

Canadian law currently bans the practice of witchcraft, sorcery, enchantment, or conjuration, and using crafty science to claim knowledge of where something that is lost may be found (Canada Criminal Code, § 365).

Border Patrol

NASA statute 14 CFR Ch. 5 (1-1-91 ed.), National Aeronautics and Space Administration, Part 1211—Extraterrestrial Exposure, was put into effect on July 16, 1969, days before man's first landing on the moon. According to the law, it was NASA policy and responsibility to "guard the Earth against any harmful contamination," and the statute focused on those who had been "extra-terrestrially exposed" or had come into contact with those so exposed.

Exposed persons were quarantined, and those not abiding by the law were subject to a fine of not more than $5,000 and prison for not more than one year, or both (18 U.S.C. 799). The statute was repealed in 1991.

I, Robot

Robots are on the march, with few laws to stop them. In the United States, there are no specific robot statutes to date, but the Occupational Safety and Health Administration (OSHA) has issued its *Guidelines for Robotic Safety*. To prevent worker injury, these guidelines require that robots move slowly, have sensitive human presence-sensing devices, and shut down immediately at the slightest hint of danger.

Robots do pose a unique danger to their fellow workers. OSHA notes robots that have lashed out with their arms and struck humans working beside them. Other workers have been crushed and spot-welded, and have even had molten aluminum poured over them. In England, at least seventy-seven workers were injured by robots in 2005 alone. Fatalities are not unknown—a Japanese robot fatally threw a factory worker against a nearby piece of machinery, and a Ford Motor Company worker was fatally struck in the head by one, while another worker was pinned and asphyxiated. No injuries have been reported at the hands of over two million Roomba vacuum robots currently in use.

Countries with more advanced robotics are responding more aggressively. Japan is drafting *Guidelines to Secure the Safe Performance of Next Generation Robots*, and South Korea's Ministry of Information, which predicts that every South Korean household will have its own robot between 2015 and 2020, is releasing the *Robot Ethics Charter*, whose guidelines are expected to substantially incorporate parts of Isaac Asimov's "Three Laws of Robotics" from his *I, Robot* series.

Sensitive issues remain. A study commissioned by England's Office of Science and Innovation cautions that robots may develop humanlike intelligence and be able to reproduce themselves and discusses the granting of robot rights in the next twenty to fifty years. It also foresees robot voting, robot taxation, and compulsory robot military service. Experts at the Swedish Royal Institute of Technology discuss the ethics of robots that contravene the Geneva Convention by firing at unarmed civilians, the sale of sex robots, and even the purchase of sex robots resembling children.

Space Cowboys

Canadians aboard the International Space Station can ignore the laws of gravity but not the laws of their native country. Canadians who commit crimes on the Space Station are subject to regular Canadian laws, as are those who commit crimes against Canadians aboard the Space Station (Canada Criminal Code, §§ 2.3, 2.31).

Waking the Dead

In Nevada, "using profane, indecent or obscene language in the presence of a dead human body" is prohibited (Nevada NRS 642.480).

UFO

Amid a spate of UFO sightings in October 1954, Mayor Lucien Juene of the well-known wine-growing town of Châteauneuf-du-Pape, France, declared a prohibition on flying saucers. The mayor issued the following decrees:

Article 1. *The overflight, the landing and the takeoff of aircraft called flying saucers or flying cigars, whatever nationality it is (sic) are prohibited on the territory of the community.*

Article 2. *Any aircraft called flying saucer or flying cigar which will land on the territory of the community will immediately be put in jail.*

Article 3. *The rural policeman and the special guard are missioned, each one in what relates to him, of the execution of this decree.*

Upside Down

"No person shall operate a reverse Bungee (*sic*) jumping ride in this state" (Nebraska Revised Statutes, § 48-1804-01).

4

Animals Among Us
(The Real Ones)

After at least fifteen thousand years of domestication and the treatment of animals as property or sometimes worse, the recent trend in animal law is to imbue even the least sentient of creatures with their own rights and protections, independent of their relationship with human beings. Some of the laws described here protect animals, others tax or even judge them, but all reveal considerably more about human nature than the animals they govern.

Animals on Trial

For hundreds of years established courts put animals on trial, according them the very highest degree of due process.

Prosecutions were commonplace and deadly serious, with witnesses called, legal texts consulted, and documents admitted into evidence. Top-notch defense attorneys would stall, contest jurisdiction, and then defend on the merits. Before trial, animals would be jailed, often alongside regular prisoners, and upon conviction be subject to the same penalties, often death. Some animals were placed on the rack to extract confessions.

Proceeding alongside these government courts were similarly elaborate religious tribunals, whose defendants were often groups of animals, like rodents, storks, eels, termites, moles, and dolphins. Typical was a 1522 trial defended by Bartholomew Chassenee, a noted legal scholar later to become the equivalent of chief justice of France. Representing a pack of rats from Autun, Chassenee first argued that the rats were not properly served with a summons, then beat the rap by citing the rats' inability to defend themselves due to their reasonable fear of being eaten by cats on the way to court.

Government trials gave animals the most equitable hearing possible, each featuring extensive investigation, the citing of past legal precedent, and the interpretation of prevailing statutes and procedures. In 1750, a she-ass was acquitted of carnal crimes. During the trial, the defense introduced a certificate signed by citizens of Vanvres, France, attesting that they had known the she-ass to have been virtuous and well behaved for over four years, never involved in scandal, and "in all habits of her life a most honest creature."

Pigs were especially susceptible to prosecution, with their disrespectful demeanor in the courtroom often held against them. In 1386, a pig in the village of Falaise, France, was tried and convicted, then dressed in men's clothes and hung in the public square. Still, fairness often prevailed. In 1379, three pigs enraged by the squealing of a porkling attacked and killed the son of a swine keeper. The three pigs were condemned to death, along with members of the entire herd who didn't participate but were convicted of being accomplices. The three perpetrators were hanged but the herd was spared.

In 1457, in Savignoy-sur-Etang, France, a sow and her six piglets were indicted, imprisoned, and tried for killing a five-year-old boy. The sow was found guilty and sentenced to hang by her hind legs from a tree, but her progeny were acquitted, due in part to their youth and also the bad example set for them by their mother. Other pigs were not so fortunate—a sow was once executed for stealing a communion wafer.

Animals, like people, were susceptible to the temptations of witchcraft and judged accordingly. In 1474, a cock was burned at the stake before a large crowd in Basel, Switzerland, after being found guilty at trial. Its crime was having laid an egg that contained a basilisk from hell.

Trials of animals were not confined to the Middle Ages. After trial in 1642 Massachusetts, a horse, a cow, two goats, various sheep, and a turkey were executed, along with their paramour, Thomas Graunger. Colonial Massachusetts also hanged two witch dogs, one for strangely afflicting anyone who fell in its gaze.

Animal trials eventually ran their course, and in at least one instance their meticulous grant of rights gave way to mob rule. In 1916, Mary the elephant, who could play twenty-five songs and astounded millions worldwide with her baseball prowess, was a top circus draw. When Mary trampled her inexperienced rider, the circus owner announced a gala execution, with kids welcome and admission free to all comers. The elephant was hung from a derrick in Erwin, Tennessee, before a crowd of twenty-five hundred, many of them children. When the chain unexpectedly snapped, Mary's cracking bones made a "right smart little racket," according to newspaper accounts of witness George Ingram, but she continued breathing and the crowd fled. The chain held the second time around, and justice was served.

The Sheep Are Worried

AN ORDINANCE FOR PREVENTING OF MISCHIEFS
ARISING FROM DOGGS IN THIS CITY

Severall Sheep having been lately worried . . . cows . . . Continually Chased and Pursued, Horses often sett upon and frightened to the great Hazard of their Rider, and the Inhabitants by their Incessant Howling and Barking in the Night time . . . all of which are Comon and Publick Nuisances and Require Preventitive and Speedy Remedy.

Be it therefore Enacted and Ordained . . . that if any Dogg or Bitch from and after the first day of November next shall Runn at anny Person . . . or Pursue any Horse or any Cow . . . It shall and may be Lawful for any Person to Kill or Destroy such Dogg or Bitch (Philadelphia City Council Ordinances, 1722).

Cow Tipping

There are no laws banning cow tipping, maybe because it doesn't really happen.

Florida, where tripping a horse with a rope is a crime (Ch. 828.12 (4)), perhaps came closest with Bill S1418 (2004), but this proposal made it a felony only to drag a cow by the tail, not to knock it over from the side; after initial success, the bill was defeated in committee.

A study led by Dr. Margo Lillie of the University of British Columbia and conducted by Tracy Boechler concludes that the classic definition of cow tipping—a few people sneaking up on a cow and pushing it over—is virtually impossible.

According to the study, a cow of 1.45 meters in height and 682 kilograms in weight pushed at an angle of 23.4 degrees relative to the ground requires 2,910 Newtons of exertion. Further, cows are soft and yielding, making them even harder to topple, and they don't sleep on their feet, just doze lightly. Thus with their keen sense of smell and hearing putting them on alert, cows will brace their knees before the first push, and the more people, the more likely an alert cow.

Physics does not preclude large mobs from attacking and knocking over cows, but such activity would then be subject to riot and conspiracy laws. Other laws exist to prevent farmers from shooting at people who knock over their cows.

Fresh Baked

In Jefferson Parish, Louisiana, all garbage, refuse, and offal—except grains—must be freshly cooked on the premises before being fed to pigs (Code of Ordinances of Jefferson Parish, § 7-187).

Animals Amore

Italy, long known for its people's lax attitude toward the law in general, has improbably become an international leader in animal rights, with the recent enactment of a spate of animal and pet protection laws:

National legislation in 2004 imposed yearlong jail sentences and fines up to €10,000 for persons who abuse or abandon their pets. That year, the city council of Reggio Emilia banned the boiling of live lobsters; mandated that "social" birds be kept in pairs; directed that all cages, coops, and hutches have rough, nonslip surfaces; and required that each pet sharing a meal got an equal portion, with fines of up to €325.

In Rome, a 2004 law bans spherical fishbowls. Karin Robertson of the Fish Empathy Project lauded the city for recognizing that "fish are interesting individuals who deserve our respect." The Roman statute also bans the docking of pet's tails and provides legal protection for those who feed stray cats.

The city of Turin now has a law fining pet owners up to €500 if they don't walk their dogs at least three times a day. A twenty-page rule book also prohibits dying a pet's fur and bans fairgrounds from giving away goldfish in plastic bags but allows walking a dog while riding a bicycle as long as the pace is slow enough not to tire the dog.

By Appointment Only

In Juneau, Alaska, no animal is allowed to enter a barbershop or establishment for the practice of hairdressing or beauty culture (Juneau, Alaska, Code of Ordinances, § 36.25.010).

Swan Song

Swans have been England's royal bird since at least 1186. Their status was further enhanced with the passage of 1482's Act of Swans, which mandated that only royalty or gentry could possess them, triggered the creation of Swanning Courts, and allowed noblemen to grab swans from yeoman and other persons of little reputation and split the profits with the king. Swans are now protected by the Wild Creatures and Forest Laws Act of 1971, which reaffirms that Her Majesty owns all swans, and royal fish, too.*

In *The Case of Swans, Trinity Term*, 34 Elizabeth I (1592), the court noted that a male swan is "a true husband to his wife" and that its monogamy caused it to "sing sweetly" at death, the famous swan song. A person caught stealing eggs out of the nest received a year and a day jail sentence, while one caught stealing an adult swan was required to hang it by the beak and give the owner enough grain to cover the head of the swan with wheat.

Currently the Queen, assisted by the Royal Master of Swans, supervisor of the yearly Swan Upping, owns all the swans in England except, arguably, those of the rebellious Orkney Islands, which follow the Viking-influenced Udal Law. The Orcadians' ability to do with swans what they wish was bolstered in 1910, when an Orkney attorney, accompanied by the procurator-fiscal, shot a swan in Harray Loch and was acquitted by the Crown's own High Court.

Not all citizens share England's swan mania. In 2005, feathers were ruffled and a battle royal ensued when Sir Peter Maxwell Davies, Master of the Queen's Music, gave the Queen the proverbial bird by eating one of the Queen's

---

*Pursuant to Statute Perogative Regis, 17 Edward II (1324), sturgeon and whales are royal fish, although we all know that a whale is really a mammal. A person caught selling a royal fish faces up to six months in prison. The Receiver of Wreck takes possession of all royal fish, although in Scotland possession accrues only if the fish is too large to be pulled ashore by six oxen. As per the *Receiver of Wreck 2004 Annual Report*, "in June a large sturgeon was caught off South Wales. . . . The Receiver contacted Buckingham Palace. . . . The Queen did not wish to exercise her right to the sturgeon."

swans. Davies claimed the swan was seared on a power line, and offered officers from the Northern Constabulary executing a search warrant at his home a taste of his swan terrine. "You take them home and you hang them for four days," he said, "and then take out the breast meat and the good leg meat, and you give the rest to the cat."

In 2006, Shamsu Miah was pinched by police in north Wales for eating a swan and sentenced to serve two months in jail. Arresting officers told Miah the swan was the property of the Queen, and he responded, "I hate the Queen, I hate this country." Trying to observe the fasting holiday of Ramadan and found with white feathers stuck to his beard and blood on his shirt, Miah told police, "I was hungry."

Swan controversies continue. In the summer of 2008 the town of Langley was terrorized for over a month when a family of swans sauntered around the village for "no apparent reason," culminating in a late June incident that forced police to block off Route A259 and seal off an adjoining shopping mall. A frustrated Trevor Weeks of East Sussex Wildlife Rescue noted that the law prohibited him from touching or moving the swans, and resigned himself to keeping a close eye on them while waiting for a license, which he said would take several weeks.

Slap That Bitch

In Minooka, Illinois, it is illegal "to suffer any bitch or slut." The section apparently refers to dogs (Minooka Village Code, § 7-1-1(Q)).

Keep Off the Grass

Article 120 of the Swiss Federal Constitution, adopted by popular vote in 1999, requires Wurde der Kratur, "account to be taken of the dignity of living beings." When the Swiss couldn't figure out what relevance that phrase had to plants, if any, they turned to the Federal Ethics Committee on Non-Human Biotechnology (ECNH) a Parliament-appointed panel of philosophers, lawyers, scientists, and theologians. They published *The Dignity of Living Beings with Regard to Plants*, subtitled *Moral Consideration of Plants for Their Own Sake*.

All panel members agreed that plants should not be harmed for no reason, and most found that plants have an inherent worth by themselves, while a few claimed that plants "strive after something" and were not to be interfered with.

The absence of a central nervous system was found not to rule out the possibility that plants have feelings, since plants have a hormonal system, react to stimuli, and can choose between various ways of "behaving." A majority could not rule out the possibility of plant "awareness," while a minority found it likely. The panel did conclude that human beings should be allowed to use plants for their own reasonable purposes, at least for now.

Ecuador is thinking bigger. In 2008, its voters approved a new constitution that made it the first country in the world to grant legal rights to an object, Nature itself, which was decreed to have the right to exist, persist, maintain, and regenerate (Title II, Fundamental Rights, Ch. 1, Rights for Nature, Art. 1).

To Dye For

In Akron, Ohio, no person shall dye or otherwise color any rabbit or baby poultry (Municipal Code of Akron, Ohio, Title 9, § 92.06).

Outfoxed

England finally passed the Hunting Act (2004), making it illegal to hunt foxes and other animals with dogs. Opposition has been stiff—a Liberty and Livelihood march against the law turned out four hundred thousand people, and legal challenges continue.

Opponents of the act claim that fox hunting actually does the foxes a favor. Five hundred members of the Royal College of Veterinary Surgeons found it the "most humane" way of treating them, as opposed to just leaving them alone, determining after careful study that being hunted down by packs of dogs and their rabid owners does not create medically "abnormal" stress. Members of the Masters of Foxhounds Association concur—they claim foxes "live in the present, unburdened by past worries and future fears," although running for one's life would appear to be more than merely a bad memory or future concern.

Hunting dogs themselves eventually become the prey, according to testimony before the House of Commons. Dogs not as bloodthirsty as their masters are shot by the kennel man, and even those that ably serve for years are shot at age six or seven, half their normal life span, at a rate of perhaps three to five thousand each year. But this is how it should be, according to a hound show press release sponsored by Fox Hunt Master Ian Farquhar, Beagle Master Dr. Mark Thomas, and Nigel Kirk of the Association of Masters of Harriers and Beagles; the release says that after five or six hunting seasons, hounds get tired and frustrated and gratefully submit to their fate when they can no longer perform their "role" in life.

Who's the Pig?

GREASED PIG CONTESTS AND TURKEY SCRAMBLES
No person shall operate, run or participate in a contest, game or other activity, in which a pig, greased, oiled or otherwise, is released and wherein the object is the capture of the pig, or in which a chicken or turkey is released or thrown into the air and wherein the object is the capture of the chicken or turkey (Minnesota Statutes, Ch. 343, § 43.16).

Ophidiophobia

Snake charmers are being squeezed by India's recent decision to begin enforcing its Wildlife Protection Act, which carries a punishment of up to three years in prison.

In 2009, five thousand charmers gathered in Kolkata, claiming the law was severely constricting their ability to make a living. Still numbering close to a million, snake charmers have established a union and hired lobbyists and now seek to be employed as snake hands at government-run snake farms.

Jerry Redfearn, not so charming, badly wanted tenant Henry Washington out of his building complex. Knowing that Washington was deathly afraid of snakes, he posed as an exterminator and used a loudspeaker to warn tenants that snakes would soon be used to get rid of mice in the building. Washington heard the announcement and fled.

Charged under Texas Penal Code Ann., § .22.07, Redfearn claimed that just threatening to release snakes in general, as opposed to poisonous snakes, was not a terrorist threat. The judges of the Texas Court of Appeals, none of them wearing a "I Hate Snakes" T-shirt in ash gray from the Ophidiophobic Anti-Snake Online Store, found that snakes were scary enough, poisonous or not, and upheld the conviction (*Redfearn v. State*, Ct. Appeals Texas, 738 S.W. 2d 28 (1987)).

Snake handling as a test of faith continues among some religious sects in the United States, chief among them the Church of God with Signs Following. Relying primarily on Mark 16:17–18—"In my name shall they cast out devils . . . They shall take up serpents; and if they drink any deadly thing, it shall not hurt them"—believers grab deadly snakes during church services and steel themselves with "salvation cocktails" of strychnine and water, sometimes followed by a lye chaser.

Snake worship is generally prohibited in the United States under cases like *Swann v. Pack*, 527 S.W. 2d 99 (Tennessee 1975), but worshipers still adhere to a higher law or sometimes to no law at all. In Alabama in 1991, snake-handling preacher Glenn Summerford forced his wife, Darlene, to stick her hand into a box of snakes. She survived, barely, and he was sentenced to ninety-nine years. Prominent snake-handling leader John Wayne Brown Jr. and his wife died of snakebite, leaving behind five children. The childrens' grandfather, a snake handler himself, promised Social Services he'd keep the kids out of church on snake night.

In 2008, pastor Gregory James Coots and nine others were arrested in Kentucky for possessing venomous snakes; a husband and wife attending his church had previously died of snakebite. Conservation officers seized more than one hundred snakes, all brought to the reptile zoo in Slade, near Natural Bridge, while an alligator discovered at the site was left where it was found.

Noisy Fowl Prohibited

In Tryon, North Carolina, pursuant to a law passed in 2006, "No person shall maintain fowl that shall crow, cackle or make any other noise that disturbs the peace and quiet of the town" (Tryon Town Ordinances, Noisy Fowl Prohibited, Ch. 91, § 91.41).

Weasel World

Mustela putorius furo, the common ferret, is welcomed in some jurisdictions, barred in others, and barely tolerated in many.

The wily weasel is banned in California pursuant to Fish and Game § 2118, and in New York City under New

York City Health Code 24 RCNY 161.01, which prohibits animals that are "wild, fierce, dangerous or naturally inclined to do harm."

Ferret fanatics, sometimes called ferrants, proudly point to a 2000 millennium celebration featuring the London Symphony Orchestra, in which ferrets were tied to little nylon harnesses and used to lay underground cable. Ferrets have also been used in oil pipelines, and in New Zealand, the Auckland local of the New Zealand Electrical Worker's Union issued a written complaint when a nonunion ferret laid wiring in sixty pipes, one 130 feet long.

Weasel worshipers in California have been driven underground by the state's law, breeding several Ferrets Anonymous organizations. At a 2009 meeting, held at an undisclosed pancake house and presided over by "President M," "Anita H" was fearful of being turned in by her neighbors while "Lance" ruminated over his ferret dwarf.

Legal battles seem to have bred a fetish for officiousness; ferret-friendly groups include the International Ferret Congress, sponsor of the yearly International Ferret Symposium, along with New York Ferret Rights Advocacy and the Ferret Emergency Response Rescue and Evacuation Team, which assists in "locating ferrets at risk, securing temporary or permanent housing . . . securing appropriate medical care and providing disaster preparedness information and resources."

The most rabid legal battles have been fought in New York City, which banned ferrets only in 1999. In *New York City Friends of Ferrets v. City of New York*, 876 F.Supp. 529, aff'd 71 F3d 405 (1995), the court upheld a city finding that ferrets were dangerous; in *1700 York Associates v. Kaskel*,

182 Misc. 2d 586 (Civil Ct. 1999), tenant Gary Kaskel fended off eviction for owning a ferret; and in *Humane Society of New York v. City of New York*, 188 Misc. 2d 735 (Supreme Court, 2001), the same Gary Kaskel was rebuffed when he tried to ferret out confidential information concerning the political posturing behind the 1999 ban.

The ferocity of New York City's ferret fandango is best reflected by a widely broadcast conversation during a 1999 radio talk show between the hapless Kaskel and Mayor Rudy Giuliani, a fearsome ferret foe not known for his sensitivity:

> [T]here's something deranged about you. The excessive concern that you have for ferrets is something you should examine with a therapist. . . . You need help. . . . This excessive concern with little weasels is a sickness. . . . [Y]ou are devoting your life to weasels. . . . I do not mean to be insulting.

Catch of the Day

The official Hawaiian state fish is the Humuhumunukunukuapua'a (Hawaii Revised Statutes, Ch. 5, § 5-11.5).

The Hartlepool Monkey

"Who hung the monkey? Hartlepool hung the monkey!" So goes the chant at a Monkeyhangers rugby game in Hartlepool, England.

At the height of the Napoleonic Wars of the early 1800s, the British were fighting against Napoleon's France, and coastal villages were on high alert. A French ship, possibly the *Chasse Maree*, sank off the eastern coast, and one bedraggled survivor washed ashore, hairy and dwarflike and dressed from head to toe in the uniform of the hated French. The castaway "spoke" in a suspiciously foreign tongue.

The presumed French spy was taken into custody, and the Hartlepool townspeople gave the spy a full-fledged trial. The mumbling defendant made a less than compelling witness in his own defense and was sentenced to be hanged, which he was.

Some say the incident never happened, but believers note that the grisly occurrence wasn't disputed at the time it was first reported, despite its great damage to the town's reputation and commercial interests. A possible explanation is that the townspeople knew the castaway was a monkey but hanged it anyway, out of sheer orneriness.

In 2002, Stuart Drummond, mascot of the Hartlepool United football team, campaigned for mayor of the now ninety-thousand-person city in a seven-foot monkey suit. Promising free bananas to all schoolchildren, he won in a landslide and, sans monkey suit, won election to two subsequent terms.

Gator Aid

In Louisiana, stealing an alligator from another, with intent to deprive the owner of the alligator, is a crime punishable by penalties ranging from not more than six months in jail and a fine of $500 or both to not more than ten years' imprisonment, with or without hard labor, and a fine of $3,000 or both. Stealing crawfish incurs the same penalties (Louisiana Code, R.S. 14:67.13 (alligators); R.S. 14:67.5 (crawfish)).

Damn Beavers

Recognized worldwide for their perseverance and industry, in 1975 beavers were accorded the highest honor ever bestowed on a rodent, being named the national animal of Canada.

Across the border, conflicting interests of beavers and people are carefully balanced. Beavers and their dams are protected by environmental statutes and federal laws that limit development near dams, but statutes also allow people to protect themselves from the occasionally aggressive eager beaver and problems like flooding, dead trees, and beaver fever.

In 1997, Michigan officials found two beaver dams in violation of a statute because they failed during a rain event and lacked permits; the beavers were ordered to cease and desist. On a larger scale, satellite imagery in 2007 uncovered a giant secret beaver dam in northern Alberta; although not yet fully operational, the dam was 2,790 feet long and 23 feet thick.

Vermont regulates its beaver battles through Title 10 V.S.A. 1272 (among others), in conjunction with *Best Management Practices for Resolving Human-Beaver Con-*

flicts in Vermont (rev. ed. 2004); vigilante activity is forbidden, and dynamite discouraged. And if conflict resolution doesn't work out, a citizen can refer to Appendix 4 of *Best Management Practices*, which provides recipes for beaver roast, beaver stew, and beaver meat loaf.

Bear Hug

In Oklahoma, bear-wrestling exhibitions are illegal, along with the declawing or removal of teeth that frequently accompanies them. Violators face a year in jail, a fine of $2,000, and may have to make restitution to any government agencies or animal cruelty societies who pay for the housing, feeding, or providing of medical treatment to the injured bears (Oklahoma Statutes, Ch. 67, § 1700).

Blackie the Talking Cat

Blackie spoke English with poise and erudition, according to Federal District Judge Bowen in his 1982 federal court decision.

Blackie's business partnership with Carl Miles and his wife began in a North Carolina rooming house. According to the sworn deposition testimony of Carl Miles, "a girl came around with a box of kittens." Upon hearing the voice of God, Miles gave Blackie a rigorous course in speech therapy. "I would tape the sounds the cat would make when he was trying to talk to me, and I would play these sounds back to him three or four hours a day. . . . He was talking when he was six months old."

Legal controversy arose because Blackie, and Miles on his behalf, accepted donations from the pedestrians in town with whom Blackie struck up conversations and because they employed talent agents to strike up business. Pursuant to Augusta's Ordinance No. 5006, various trades and businesses had to pay licensing taxes, and although Judge Bowen found that "the ordinance does not provide for the licensing of a talking cat," section 2 of the law did require any "Agent or Agency not specifically mentioned" to pay a $50 tax.

When the city tried to tax Blackie, Miles objected, claiming that he and they were not engaged in an "occupation" of the sort listed by the ordinance, and that the catchall phrase "not specifically mentioned" was unconstitutionally vague and overbroad. The Eleventh Circuit Court of Appeals found against Blackie on the tax issue and also rejected his free speech claim, finding that he was not considered a person as defined by the Bill of Rights and that, in any case, "Blackie can clearly speak for himself" (*Miles v. City Council of Augusta, Georgia*, 551 F.Supp. 349 (S.D. Ga. 1982); affirmed U.S. Court of Appeals, Eleventh Circuit, 710 F.2d 1542 (1983)).

The Camel Cavalry

On March 3, 1855, Congress passed a statute establishing the U.S. Camel Corps. The camels were shipped from North Africa and adapted well initially, but the program was eventually scrapped because the unyielding ungulates proved to be stubborn and aggressive, and they frightened the horses.

Pigs in Play

Once and for all, the law does not require that European pigs be given footballs and basketballs to play with, according to miffed European Union officials.

EU Council Directive 2001/88/EC and Commission Directive 2001/93/EC, amending Directive 91/630/EEC, require that pigs be given "manipulable materials," with violations of the directives resulting in thousand-pound fines or more. Misunderstanding arose when the official spokesperson of the UK Department of Environment, Food and Rural Affairs (DEFRA) said, "We mean footballs and basketballs. Farmers may also need to change the balls so the pigs don't get tired with the same one. Different colour ones will do."

When the comments caused an uproar, British European Commission head Jim Dougal protested vehemently: "There is no mention of toys in the EU Directive."

Warminster pig farmer Neville Warner said his piglets seemed quite pleased with a plastic airplane and a furry gray teddy bear.

Shark v. Shark

The Shark Finning Prohibition Act (U.S.C. § 1857 (2002)) makes it illegal to remove the fins of a shark and then throw the carcass into the sea, or to have a shark fin on board a boat without the rest of the shark. The act applies to all U.S. citizens and also prohibits foreign vessels and fishermen from shark finning in U.S. ports and economic zones.

Because the fins are used in shark fin soup and sell for $300 a pound but shark meat is practically worthless, fishermen cut off the fins and then throw the often still-living shark back in the water, to sink to the bottom, bleed to death, or be eaten.

Stomping the Fish

In 2003, Emilie Martinez slept on the sofa of the Brooklyn apartment where she lived with her three children; boyfriend, Garcia; two dogs; a cat; and three goldfish, each named after one of the children.

She awoke to find Garcia throwing the aquarium into the television set. "That could have been you," he said. When nine-year-old Juan heard the commotion and came running out of his bedroom, Garcia stomped on and killed his beloved namesake, Juan the goldfish.

Garcia was arrested for assault and also aggravated cruelty to animals, a felony under Agriculture and Markets Law 353-a(1), which holds guilty a person who kills a "companion animal."

At trial, Garcia's attorney argued that his client should be charged with a misdemeanor, not a felony, claiming that a mere goldfish could not possibly be considered a companion animal.

Found guilty at trial, an appeals court noted that a gold-fish did meet the felony statute's "mutual affection" requirement, but more troublesome was Garcia's claim that a fish could not be a companion animal because it wasn't domesticated, another of the statute's requirements.

Garcia's attorney cited 4 Am. Jur. 2d, Animals, § 2, which defined domesticated animals as those which "no longer possess the disposition or inclination to escape," and announced that "if dropped in a pond . . . a goldfish will do so [escape] without any hesitation and will not look back."

But the court rejected the argument, finding that gerbils, hamsters, guinea pigs, and rabbits would escape if given half the chance but were still commonly considered "domesticated" pets.

Fish and people-stomper Garcia was sentenced to five and a half to eleven years in prison (*People v. Garcia, New York First Dept.*, 29 A.D.3d 255 (2006)).

Passports for Pets

Jet-setting pets now breeze through customs with pet passports, recently accepted by members of the European Union and informally adopted by the United States and several other countries.

Under EC Regulation 998/2003, thousands of progressive pets now whisk across borders hassle free, though many countries are still adding or subtracting their own rules. Virtually all European countries and the United States require the passport to confirm rabies vaccination and owner information, and most require the pet to have an identifying microchip implanted under its skin.

Meanwhile, guinea pigs are entitled to a transport container with an interior height of at least six inches for those weighing up to five hundred grams and a floor space measuring no less than 290.3 square centimeters, while dwarf hamsters can luxuriate under high ceilings of 12.7 centimeters and larger hamsters 15.2 centimeters (Code of Federal Regulations (CFR), Title 9, § 3.36). A nursing female hamster and her brood are required by law to be given private living accommodations (9 CFR, Ch. 1).

Romancing the Reptile

In Illinois, a person selling a reptile must give written notice to the buyer: "Don't nuzzle or kiss your pet reptile" (Illinois Compiled Statutes, Animal Welfare Act, § 18.1(b)(2)(D)).

Step Lively

The deliberate "soring" of horses, the Tennessee Walking Horse in particular, triggered passage in 1970 of the Horse Protection Act, 15 U.S.C. §§ 1821–1831 (Amended 2000).

The Walking Horse is valued for its smooth gait, and the act bans the practice of inflicting pain to the horse's foot to cause it to raise its front legs higher than normal to achieve the desired Big Lick gait.

Among the banned techniques are burning and cutting, application of blistering agents, and the use of tacks, nails, and screws. Other procedures include overtrimming of the hooves, too-tight shoeing, wrapping the feet in chemical-soaked wraps, and the use of kerosene and mustard oil.

The temptation is apparently fierce: as of 1999, nine of the last eleven presidents of the Walking Horse Trainers Association and nine of sixteen winners of the Trainer of the Year Award had been ticketed, suspended, or convicted. A 2002 article in the *Kentucky Law Journal* (90 KY.L.J. 661) notes a 2001 horse show where 140 of the 200 expected entrants suddenly dropped out when threatened with strict enforcement.

But every summer, two thousand horses at the Tennessee Walking Horse National Celebration do the high step, whether they want to or not.

Fatt Cattle

AN ACT TO PREVENT THE SELLING OF LIVE FATT
CATLE BY BUTCHERS (1663)
[I]t is enacted that noe person using the Craft or Mistery of a Butcher should buy any fatt Oxen, Steeres Runts Kine Heifers Calves or sheepe and sell the same againe alive.

Animals Ascendant

In 2008, the European Commission adopted a proposal to expand the scope of animal rights throughout the European Union. Focusing on animals used in scientific experiments, the proposal went into effect in 2010. Momentum for the changes came from widely publicized stories of animal suffering, chief among them the continuing saga of Matthias "Hiasl" Pan.

In 1982, Hiasl, a chimpanzee, saw his mother shot by poachers and was ripped from her dead body. Stuffed into a box, he was sold in Austria for the equivalent of €33,000 to Immuno, an Austrian pharmaceutical company. While on his way to Vienna, Hiasl and his handlers were intercepted by tipped-off activists and customs officers, who found the chimp lacked newly required documentation.

Hiasl was eventually taken in by a human family and raised as their own, as legal wrangling ensued between Hiasl supporters and the drug company. But in 2005, the Austrian parliament voted unanimously to ban all experiments on apes and monkeys, and the drug company gave up its claim.

The case took another turn in 2006, when twenty-five-year-old Hiasl, now in his prime, was threatened with homelessness. Supporters sued to have Hiasl declared a "person" under Austrian law, their petition supported by experts in science, philosophy, law, and anthropology. The petition was denied, and Hiasl has since applied for leave to appeal before the European Court of Human Rights.

With recent amendments to EU Directive 86/609/EEC,

other lab animals in Europe might have things easier. Provisions address everyday issues like humidity and bedding material; ensure that animals are given a degree of control over their environment and appropriate "enrichment techniques"; and guarantee animals the right to personal, emotional, and intellectual growth.

Among the animals getting species-specific protection are the Mongolian gerbil, the Syrian hamster, vervets, and aquatic urodeles (whose length for fitting must be measured from snout to vent). Pigeons are guaranteed short flights, and geese a minimum pond size.

Counting Sheep

In Wales, pastoral images of a shepherd and his dog tending their woolly flock in a verdant green meadow no longer hold true, not since the passage of Welsh Statutory Instrument, 2006, No. 1036 (W.106), the Sheep and Goats (Records, Identification, and Movement) Order (2006).

Under the instrument, the moving and tagging of all ovine and caprine animals, otherwise known as sheep and goats, must be accomplished pursuant to a thirty-six-page-long set of rules. A typical rule concerning the transport of sheep and goats reads:

7(2) The provisions of Schedule 1 apply in addition to the requirements of—

(a) Articles 4(1), 4(2)(a), 4(4), 4(5), and 4(6) of the Council Regulation and this Part of this Order; (b) Articles

5(1), 5(3), and 5(5) of the Council Regulation and Part 3 of this Order; and

(c) Articles 6(1) and 6(3) of the Council Regulation and Part 4 of this Order.

Also, the use of red ear tags is strictly limited, and a person may not attach an additional ear tag to a goat or sheep that already has three ear tags.

Poop Patrol

DNA data will connect poop to pooch in Petah Tikva, Israel.

In 2008, the city embarked on a pilot sanitation program that matches dropping to dog by having owners bring their pets to a municipal vet, who swabs their cheek for DNA and enters the data into a central registry. Owners who then drop their packages into designated bins are given credits through DNA matching and become eligible for free dog food and treats. When registration in the program becomes mandatory, droppings found on the street will be traced back to their owner, with an accompanying fine.

Rules of the Roost

Faced with a financial meltdown and massive layoffs, in September 2009 the Los Angeles City Council passed a resolution limiting roosters to one per household. Los Angeles follows in the footsteps of Riverside County, California, which in August 2009 amended its rooster ordinance to require those keeping seven or more crowing roosters age two months or older in a soundproof enclosure between sunset and sunrise (Riverdale County Ordinance 817, § 1).

5

Life's Essentials
Food and Sex

We and the laws we live by have come a long way since the days of Sumeria and the Middle Ages, but people haven't really changed, and our daily needs and urges remain the same. So these days we have our equivalents of the medieval Assize of Bread and more than our share of bawdy laws and scarlet letters. This chapter focuses on a few of the odder laws governing our needs and pleasures, from ketchup to kissing, and illustrates some of the sillier and pettiest statutes conceived by self-appointed taste-makers and moral guardians.

Pizza Police

Pizza with pineapples? That's a cake.
— Alfonso Cucciniello, Da Michelle pizzeria, Naples

In 2004, Naples passed laws mandating exactly how an "official" Neapolitan pie must be made. Among the rules:

1. Diameter cannot exceed 35 centimeters, and must be round.
2. Must use bufala mozzarella only.
3. Must be baked in a wooden oven at 905 degrees Fahrenheit.
4. Dough must be "soft, elastic and not sticky."
5. Must use plum tomatoes.
6. Pizza must be no thicker than 2.5 millimeters in middle, with crust of 2 centimeters.

And, of course, absolutely no MeatZZFeast, Vegorama, or Meatosaurus pizzas.*

Kissing

Kissing has been outlawed through the ages, for all sorts of reasons.

Roman emperor Tiberius outlawed kissing in public ceremonies to prevent a plague of fever blisters. Public kissing was also outlawed in Naples in 1562, supposedly punishable by death, and kissing in public was banned in 1699 Puritan New England. "If you kiss a woman in pulick . . . if any information is given to the Select Members, both shall be whipt or fined."

*Registered trademarks of Domino's Pizza.

In 1439, England's Parliament petitioned to be excused from kissing Henry VI, presenting the Petition from Commons to Be Excused from Kissing the King Because of the Plague: "pestilence . . . more comunely reyneth than hath bien usuell . . . desirying the helth and welfare of your most noble person . . . in the doying of their said homage may omitted the said kissying of you."

Health-based anti-kissing laws continue. In 2009, Mexico warned against kissing to prevent the spread of swine flu, while Hong Kong in 2005 issued warnings against kissing pet parrots and birds. More dubiously, the town of Adana, Turkey, has banned public kissing between two men but not between a man and a woman or even two women, claiming it's unhygienic in the summer heat.

Health concerns aside, authorities worldwide are now rushing to outlaw kissing just because they don't want people to kiss. In South Africa, kissing between teens younger than sixteen was prohibited in 2008, resulting in a protest, drawing thousands of smooching teenagers in Johannesburg. According to Natalie Winston, age twelve, "We're young, we need to experiment. When you're twenty-one, you're old already, and ugly."

Kissing has also recently been banned in England's Warrington train station; to keep pedestrian traffic moving, Ghostbuster-like no-kissing signs—red slash through a silhouetted couple—have been posted. In Italy, the mayor of Eboli will fine couples kissing in cars €500.

Guanajuato, Mexico, has been a kissing battleground. The mayor and city council outlawed public kissing and other displays of affection, but after large and affectionate protests in front of city hall, city officials succumbed to popular opinion and "froze" the law. The mayor even went a step further and publicly declared Guanajuato the "Kissing Capital of the World."

Forbidden Fruit

A durian's smell is so strong and stinky that it is banned from Southeast Asian Airlines, hotels, and public transport. Signs showing the spiky, football-size fruit with a slash through it appear in Singapore subways, announcing a $500 fine for possession.

California Dreaming

In California, "no vendor shall vend stuffed articles depicting the female breasts (sold as "boobie pillows") within one thousand (1,000) feet of any county highway" (California—Offenses Against Public Decency, § 9.12.010).

Violation of the boobie pillows statute warrants a fine and/or imprisonment in the county jail for not more than ninety days and a fine of not more than $500 or both.

Wisconsin

Wisconsin likes butter, hates margarine, and takes cheese very seriously, according to various laws still on the books.

Pursuant to Wisconsin Statutes, Food Regulation 97.18

(in effect from 1977), serving butter-colored margarine in a restaurant is a criminal offense unless ordered by a customer, with penalties of up to three months in jail for a first offense and a year for a second (97.18(4)). Margarine cannot be served to students, patients, or prisoners (97.18(5)).

Margarine can be sold only in pound chunks, no less (97.18(3)(b)), with the word *margarine* set off in big print (97.18(3)(c)). Margarine masquerading as butter is defined as having a tint containing "more than 1–6/10 degrees of yellow or yellow and red collectively, but with an excess of yellow over red" (97.18(1)(b)).

Laws are strictly enforced by trained and licensed butter graders (97.175). Refrigerator magnets saying, "No Thanks, I'm Having Butter" are available from the Wisconsin Historical Society.

According to laws put in effect in 1993, Wisconsin Cheddar must be "highly pleasing" (Agriculture, Trade and Consumer Protection, 81.40(1)), while brick and muenster must be free from sweet holes but can have a very slight feed flavor (81.60(1)), and baby Swiss requires well-developed eyes (81.91(1)).

The flavor of colby and Monterey Jack must be both fine and highly pleasing but is allowed to be lacking in flavor development (81.50(1)). In bandaged cheeses, the bandage shall not be wrinkled, burst, or torn, and the cheese shall not be lopsided or huffing (81.40(4)(a)). All flavors and tastes must be determined organoleptically.

Foods besides butter and cheese *are* eaten in Wisconsin. Pursuant to a statute passed in 2007, a "meal" is a diversified selection of food products that are customarily consumed as breakfast, lunch, and dinner; cannot be easily eaten without accompanying tableware; and may not be conveniently consumed while standing or walking (Taxation 77.54(20)(bg)1). A "sandwich" is a food that consists of a filling that is placed between slices of bread, pursuant to a 2009 law (77.54(2)(bg)2.b), and sale of fish flour is allowed with appropriate labeling (Wisconsin Statutes 97.13).

A New Beginning

In 2002, Brazil finally repealed a 1916 law allowing Brazilian men (only) to annul their marriage if, within ten days of the wedding, they discovered their new wife was not a virgin (Brazil Civil Code).

Sticky Situation

Years of delicate diplomacy have resulted in a partial lifting of the infamous chewing gum ban in Singapore, leaving a single curious exception.

Import and sale of gum has been banned since 1992 under the Control of Manufacture and Sale of Food Acts, after gumming up the works of keyholes, elevator buttons, and subway door sensors. Lee Kuan Yew, father of the country, recounts in his memoirs, "ministers who had studied in America recounted how the underside of lecture theater seats were filthy with chewing gum stuck to them like barnacles."

But after two and a half years of negotiations, President Clinton and former U.S. congressman and lobbyist Phil

Crane finally achieved a partial lifting of the ban as part of a free trade agreement, so that gum companies like Wrigley's could open a new market.

Now gum can be sold, but only for "medicinal" or "therapeutic" purposes, an exception conveniently leaving room for gum like Wrigley's Orbit, with calcium lactate to strengthen enamel. The gum can be sold only by dentists and pharmacists, with all sales registered and names taken. Smuggling gum into the country carries a one-year jail sentence.

So far no political superpowers or corporate sponsors have stepped forward to try to modify similar Singapore statutes concerning spitting and failing to flush toilets, both of which carry heavy fines.

Pretty, Please

17-31—MALE DRESSING AS FEMALE
"No man or boy shall dress as a girl or woman without a permit from the sheriff" (Walnut City (California) Code, Title III, Public Health and Safety).

The Rots

In New Jersey, "no person shall operate or conduct an establishment where the business of breaking eggs is carried on without a license. No egg shall be broken for use as food that has decomposed to such an extent that it has a putrefactive odor and is therefore of that grade commonly known as "rots" or that is wholly or partially decomposed, moldy, or sour or that is partially hatched or contains blood rings or veins (New Jersey Statutes, § 24:11-1, 3 (1966)).

Yield

Pursuant to a Kentucky law repealed in 1975, any person appearing in ordinary bathing garb on the highway or street of any city without police protection was subject to a fine of not less than $5 or more than $25 (Kentucky Acts/ Revised Statutes, Offenses Against Morality, § 436.140; repealed January 1, 1975).

Curvy Cucumbers

In July 2009, European Union bureaucrats yielded to public pressure and repealed detailed statutes concerning the shape, size, and color of asparagus (must be green for 80 percent of its length), Brussels sprouts, cabbage, and twenty-three other fruits and vegetables.

The laws exasperated both buyers and sellers; England's Sainsbury's supermarket chain withdrew a Halloween promotion featuring imperfect fruits and vegetables for fear produce managers would be arrested as criminals, and then fought back with a "Save Our Ugly Fruit and Vegetables" campaign.

"This marks a new dawn for the curvy cucumber and

the knobby carrot," said the European commissioner of agriculture, speaking of the demise of laws like EC 730/1999 (forked carrots prohibited) and EC 85/2004 (no apples under fifty millimeters in diameter).

Typical of the standards was that for cucumbers, pursuant to Commission Regulation (EEC) 1677/88:

> *Having regard to Council Regulations (EEC) No 1035/72 of 18 May 1972 . . . as last amended by Regulation (EEC) No 1117/88(2), and in particular Article 2(3) thereof. . . . Whereas such changes entail alteration of the supplementary quality class as laid down by Council Regulation (EEC) No 1194/69(4) as last amended by Regulation (EEC) No 79/88(5) . . . in accordance with the opinion of the Management Committee for Fruits and Vegetables. . . .*
>
> *Article 1—the quality standards for cucumbers falling within subheading 0707 11 and 0707 00 19 of the combined nomenclature shall be set out in the Annex thereto. These standards shall apply . . . under the conditions laid down in Regulation (EEC) No 1035/72.*
>
> *Article 2—Regulation No 183/64/EEC is hereby amended as follows:—the second indent of Article 1(2) is deleted, Annex 1/2 is deleted.*
>
> *Article 3—Regulation (EEC) No 1194/69 is hereby amended . . . in Article 1, the words "and cucumbers" are deleted.*

Pursuant to the law Class 1 cucumbers had to be well shaped and straight ("maximum height of the arc: 10 mm per 10 cm of the length of the cucumber"). Gherkins were exempted.

The repeal does not extend to bananas, which must still be

free from abnormal curvature, though Class 1 bananas can have slight defects of shape. As an EU spokesperson grudgingly conceded, "a curve is a normal shape for a banana."

This wasn't the first food fight in the EU's contentious history. Greece quarreled with Denmark when the Danes tried to sell feta cheese, and the Danes successfully resisted an EU ban of their beloved Queen Bridgette apple, deemed too small for Eurocrat palates. Similar skirmishes have erupted over gouda and sherry.

EU chocolate has been especially controversial. Traditionally made with cocoa butter, England successfully demanded that cheaper vegetable fat be allowed as a substitute, and a 2000 chocolate directive for the first time allowed England to export the cheaper chocolate to other EU members. Parisians were appalled as Mars Bars and Kit Kats flooded the city in place of their beloved crillo (delicate yet complex, rich secondary notes) and Gianduja (nutty, slightly gritty), and protested by picketing EU headquarters in Brussels.

Godiva sniffed that only chocolate with cocoa butter should be considered real chocolate, while the more commercial Cadbury urged chocolate snobs to lighten up and "celebrate Europe's diversity."

Teflon

In Minnesota restaurants, pans with nonstick coatings can be washed only by using nonabrasive sponges or utensils (Minnesota Administrative Rules, Nonstick Coatings, § 4626.0493).

No Petting

Walking the dog is no longer a babe magnet for Saudi men, pursuant to a 2008 law banning men from walking dogs in public.

Concerned at "the rising phenomenon of men using cats and dogs to make passes at women," Saudi authorities who catch men outside with a cat or dog will confiscate the pets and force the owner to sign a written admission. The law is enforced by the Commission for the Promotion of Virtue and Prevention of Vice.

Bon Apetit

A Food and Drug Administration booklet called *The Food Defect Action Levels* sets forth guidelines for "Natural or unavoidable defects in food for human use that present no health hazard." The booklet provides definitions of commonly found food contaminants, the presence of which are all perfectly acceptable. The following items are commonly found in the foods we eat and are considered safe at "reasonable" levels:

Copepods. *Small, free-swimming marine crustaceans, many of which are fish parasites. In some species, the females enter the tissues of host fish and may form pus pockets.*

Foreign matter. *"[O]bjectionable matter such as sticks, stones, burlap bagging, cigarette butts, etc."*

Infestation. *The presence of any live or dead life cycle stages of insects in a host product (for example, weevils in pecans, fly eggs and maggots in tomato products) or evidence of their presence (excreta, cast skins, chewed product residues, urine, etc.) or the establishment of an active breeding population.*

Whole or equivalent insect. *A whole insect, or body portions with head attached.*

If typically prepared foodstuffs have Food Defect Action Levels below the thresholds noted here, they are deemed acceptable:

Asparagus. *Insect filth—10 percent by count of spears or pieces are infested with six or more attached beetle eggs and/or sacs.*

Mushrooms. *Average of over 20 or more maggots of any size per 100 grams of drained mushrooms. Average of 75 mites per 100 grams drained.*

Eggs. *Direct microscopic counts of 5 million or more bacteria per gram.*

Macaroni and noodle products. *Average of 225 insect fragments or more per 225 grams, average of more than 4.5 rodent hairs or more per 225 grams.*

Tomato paste and other sauces. *Average of 30 or more fly eggs per 100 grams or 15 or more fly eggs and 1 or more maggots per 100 grams.*

Chocolate. *Average is 60 or more insect fragments per 100 grams or any one subsample containing 90 or more insect fragments.*

Coffee beans. *If live external infestation is present one is to use the Compliance Policy Guide titled* Food Storage and Warehousing-Adulteration-Filth *"in accordance with 'Interpretation of Insect Filth.'"*

Cinnamon. *Average of 1 milligram or more mammalian excreta per pound (Food Defect Action Level, Title 21, Ch. 1, Subch. B, Part 110, Subpart G, § 110.110).*

No Flirting

In Haddon Township, New Jersey, a person may not approach another person of the opposite sex in a public place and by word, sign, or gesture attempt to become acquainted with that person against their will, or attempt to entice them into doing any indecent or unnatural act (Haddon Township Code Ordinances, § 175-12).

The Law of the Sea

A person inspecting fish or frog legs in the European Union better hit the law books before donning a smock.

CHAPTER II(4) OF § VIII OF ANNEX III TO
REGULATION (EC) NO. 853/2004
The visual inspection of fish fillets or fish slices must be carried out by qualified persons during trimming and after filleting or slicing. Where an individual examina-

tion is not possible because of the size of the fillets or the filleting operations, a sample plan must be drawn up and kept available for the competent authority.

ANNEX II, FISHERY PRODUCTS, § 1, CHAPTER II (2)
Those handling frogs legs must sign a declaration pursuant to Appendix I to Annex VI (Frog's Legs and Snails), Part A:

I the undersigned declare that I am aware of the relevant provisions of Regulation (EC) No. 178/2002 (EC) No. 852/2004 and (EC) No. 853 /2004 and certify that the frogs legs described above were produced in accordance with those requirements; in particular, that they came from establishments implementing a programme based on the HACCP principles in accordance with Regulation (EC) No. 852/2004 and originate from frogs that have been bled, prepared and where appropriate, chilled, frozen, or processed in a hygienic manner. . . . The colour of the stamp and signature must be different from that of the other particulars in the certificate.

The Ballings of the Wort

A record of the ballings of the wort must be kept by a brewer (Alcohol, Tobacco and Firearms, Title 27, § 25.293).

Bold and Spicy

U.S. Department of Agriculture (USDA) authorized Commercial Item Descriptions (CID) to help ensure that hardworking government employees get the condiments they deserve:

For their protection the list of seven official ketchup flavors for government employee use has "jalapeno" divided into three subcategories, and government-approved "smooth" texture *does* take into account stray bits of onions, although on taste there can be no compromise.

CLASSIFICATION
Flavor I—Garlic
Flavor II—Habanero
Flavor III—Mesquite
Flavor IV—Smoke
Flavor V—Jalapeno
   Style A—Mild
   Style B—Medium
   Style C—Hot
Flavor VI—Chipotle
Flavor VII—Other

5.3 TEXTURE

The flavored catsup shall be smooth. . . . All spices and seasonings shall be uniformly comminuted and distributed, except that pieces of spices, onion and chili peppers may be present.

5.4 FLAVOR AND ODOR

The flavored catsup shall have a spicy, sweet, slightly tangy, cooked tomato flavor and odor.

Strict regulation also ensures that catsup served in government cafeterias comes out of the bottle neither too fast nor too slow:

> *The consistency of the finished food is such that its flow is not more than 14 centimeters in 30 seconds at 20 degrees C when tested in a Bostwick Consistometer.... The trough must also be at a temperature close to 20 degrees C. Adjust end-to-end level of Bostwick Consistometer by means of the spirit level. . . . Fill the chamber . . . avoiding air bubbles. . . . Pass a straight edge across the top of chamber. . . . Immediately start the stopwatch . . . repeat a third time.*

On the other side of the condiment aisle, as of May 29, 2007, Mustard Metric A-A 20036C supersedes Mustard Metric A-A-20036B and yellow, spicy brown, Dijon, honey, stone-ground, horseradish, deli, and "other" mustard may now be served to hungry government bureaucrats throughout the land. Yellow shall be of smooth consistency and mild flavor, Dijon must hit mild white wine notes, and horseradish shall have visible specks and a pungent, hot, and spicy flavor. Testing and laboratory analysis of all officially approved mustard flavors shall be done in accordance with the Official Methods of Analysis of the AOAC International (21 C.F.R. § 155.194—Catsup).

Swill Milk

In colonial times New York City cows grazed in public pastures and squares right in the middle of town. But the cows were gradually pushed farther away in favor of people, and without refrigeration it became increasingly difficult for farmers to transport milk to customers without spoilage.

Beginning in the 1820s, farmers solved the problem by renting crowded stalls next to liquor distilleries, feeding their diseased cattle discarded whiskey slop, and producing swill milk:

> On opening the doors of these foul prison houses, midnight darkness, and a hot pestilential vapor arrested our progress . . . filth and wretchedness that beggars all attempts at description . . . an acrid swill. . . . The milk of these animals . . . is daily served in their tea and coffee as "Pure Orange County Milk."
>
> Henry Bengh, Letter to the New York Times, January 14, 1869:
>
> [A] huge distillery, sending out its tartarian fumes . . . [cows] huddled close together . . . appendages and troughs to conduct and receive the hot slush from the still with which to gorge the stomachs of these unfortunate animals . . . the hot steam of whiskey slop, loaded with carbonic acid gas.
>
> —Robert Hartley, children's rights advocate, "An Historical, Scientific and Practical Essay on Milk," 1842

What resulted was milk that was thin and blue, and often doctored with starch, plaster, or chalk. According to the *Report of the Select Committee of the Board of Health* (1858), swill milk caused diarrhea, dysentery, cholera, and a virtual "holocaust of children."

During one city inspection of a swill milk plant in Manhattan, eighty-six cows, many tailless, were found in a dilapidated building. When the manager threatened to sic his bulldog on the inspectors, Dr. Cyrus Edison pulled out his revolver and said he'd be glad to use it.

In 1873–1875, laws were finally passed that banned the sale of swill milk from distillery-fed cows.

I'm a Lumberjack and I'm Okay

Rugged Canadians don't like to talk about it: "A citizen is subject to prosecution if without justification he or she advertises or publishes information about . . . a method for restoring sexual virility (Canada Criminal Code, § 163 (Corrupting Morals)).

Fruit or Vegetable?

The Supreme Court case of *Nix v. Heddon* (1893) held that tomatoes are a vegetable, not a fruit, based on a carefully reasoned analysis of their rightful place in soups, desserts, and as a welcome companion to fish and meats.

The case arose from a disputed interpretation of the Tariff Act of 1883, which required that tax be paid on imported vegetables but not on fruit. Nix claimed that tomatoes were a fruit and therefore not taxable, but tax collector Heddon claimed that tomatoes were a vegetable.

At trial, the Nix attorney read the definition of *fruit* and *vegetable* from three different dictionaries, and his two expert witnesses discussed the implications of cabbage, cauliflower, turnips, potatoes, peas, and beans. Heddon's attorney countered by reading his own definitions of peas, eggplant, cucumber, squash, and peppers, with Nix's attorney then responding with yet more definitions, this time of parsnips and carrots.*

The Supreme Court decided in favor of the tax collector, finding that the tomato's use in savory meals made it a vegetable, not a fruit, and declaring that tomatoes are "usually served at dinner in, with or after the soup, fish or meats which constitute the principal part of the repast, and not, like fruits, generally, as dessert" (*Nix v. Heddon*, 149 U.S. 304).

In 2005, New Jersey cited the *Nix* case, along with the tomato's "legendary flavor," as a basis for designating the tomato the official state vegetable (State of New Jersey, 212th Legislature, No. A1210).

Overexposed

St. John's County, Florida, has succeeded in making nudity grossly unattractive:

*Pursuant to European Union Council Directive 2001/113/EC of 2001, carrots can now be defined as a fruit as well as a vegetable.

DEFINITIONS:

b. Breast: A portion of the human female mammary gland (commonly referred to as the female breast) including the nipple and the areola (the darker colored area of the breast surrounding the nipple) and an outside area of such gland wherein such outside area is (i) reasonably compact and contiguous to the areola and (ii) contains at least the nipple and the areola and 1/4 of the outside surface area of such gland.

c. Buttocks: The area at the rear of the human body (sometimes referred to as the glutaeus maximus) which lies between two imaginary straight lines running parallel to the ground when a person is standing, the first or top such line being 1/2 inch below the top of the vertical cleavage of the nates . . . and the second or bottom such line being 1/2 inch above the lowest point of the curvature of the fleshy protuberance (sometimes referred to as the gluteal fold), and between two imaginary straight lines, one on each side of the body (the "outside lines"), which outside lines are perpendicular to the ground and to the horizontal lines described above. . . .

Notwithstanding the above, Buttocks shall not include the leg, the hamstring muscle below the gluteal fold, the tensor fasciae lathe muscle or any of the above-described portion of the human body that is between either (i) the left inside perpendicular line and the left outside perpendicular line or (ii) the right inside perpendicular line and the right outside perpendicular line.

For the purpose of the previous sentence the left in-side perpendicular line shall be an imaginary straight line on the left side of the anus (i) that is perpendicular to the ground and to the horizontal lines described above and (ii) that is 1/3 of the distance from the anus to the left outside line.

Section 8. Enforcement and Penalties: . . . upon con-viction shall be punished by a fine not to exceed $500 or by imprisonment in the County jail not to exceed 60 days or by both such fine and imprisonment.

Justice by the Jar

With a name like Smucker's, what's on the label better be in the jar.

In 1987, Smucker's began selling its Simply 100% Fruit line of jams, but years later, buyers and their class action attorneys claimed the jams weren't filled with 100 percent fruit. The jams were composed mostly of syrup, juice concentrates, pectin, and other ingredients; the blueberry jam contained only 43 percent blueberries and the strawberry only 33 percent strawberries.

The company claimed every ingredient was clearly listed on the label and that all ingredients were natural and "fruit-related."

This and other similar cases settled, and now Smucker's labels say the product is sweetened with other, all natural ingredients (*Smith v. J.M. Smucker Co.*, No. 03CHO8522, Illinois Cir. Ct. (2006)).

Mardi Gras

In Louisiana, one who prepares jambalaya, hard- and soft-shell crabs, *cochon de lait*, and Italian food need not follow the state sanitary code as long as the food is prepared in what the statute calls "the traditional manner" (Louisiana Codes, Public Health and Safety, RS 40:4.2).

Last Supper

After a storm in 1884, English sailors Dudley, Stephens, Brooks, and Richard Parker* were cast adrift in a small boat. Over the course of twenty days, they had virtually no water and ate two tins of turnips and a small turtle. Days from death, Dudley and Stephens killed and ate the weaker Parker, and drank his fresh blood. Four days later they were rescued.

A British court rejected their plea of necessity and sentenced them to death for murder, but with a recommendation of mercy, and ultimately sentenced them to six months in prison (*R v. Dudley and Stephens*, 14 QBD 273 (1884)).

---

*In 1974, noted author and intellectual Arthur Koestler sponsored a contest seeking the greatest coincidence in world history. The winner featured Edgar Allan Poe's only novel, *The Narrative of Arthur Gordon Pym of Nantucket*, published decades before this incident. The novel described the plight of four stranded shipmates, three of whom ate the fourth. The unfortunate fourth was named Richard Parker.

Happy Couple

In Florida, *married* partners who engage in open and gross lewdness or lascivious behavior together, as well as those not married, are guilty of a misdemeanor in the second degree (Florida Statutes, Title XLVI, Ch. 798, § 798.02).

In 1995, the "lewd or lascivious" portion of the statute was challenged by two women arrested for performing "their own unique form of entertainment," and the case against them was dismissed by a trial court concerned that even innocent behavior like "a come hither look" could be prosecuted, but the arrest was reinstated on appeal (*State of Florida v. Tiffany Cara Coyle and Cherry Che Flatley*, District Court of Appeal of Florida, Second District Case No. 96-04073 (1998)).

Free Trade

> *[E]xpanded trade benefits all peoples in all nations, lifting lives and hopes all across the world.*
> —President Clinton farewell address (2001)

A massive bureaucratic structure has been established to facilitate the free flow of goods and services around the world, including the 1989 *Harmonized Tariff Schedule of the United States* (HTS), describing all goods in trade. Based on the *International Harmonized Commodity Description and Coding System*, it is administered by the World Customs Organization in Brussels, and classification must be done in accordance with the General and Additional U.S. Rules of Interpretation.

Below are examples taken from the *Tariff Schedule*:

*Tariff No. 1704.90.3505; 9503.49.0020; 9801.00.1096 (1997)—**Mr. Potato Head**—China—Mr. Potato Head container filled with 30 grams of small candies-Harmonized Tariff Schedule of the United States (HTS)—toys not having a spring mechanism.*

*Tariff No. 1704.90.3505; 9801.00.1098 (1996)—**Pez Candy Dispenser**—China—plastic Pez dispenser capable of holding six pieces of Pez candy, attached to metal key ring and packaged with two .29 ounce rolls of Pez candy. Part 177, Customs Regulations (19 C.F.R. 177).*

*Tariff No. 1704.90.3505; 1806.90.9010 (1996)—**Ooozy Pops**—Mexico—hollow plastic tube which holds 0.9 ounces of liquid candy syrup or sauce. The product is consumed by removing the plastic cap from the lollipop and turning a screw. Customs Regulations (19 C.F.R. 177).*

*Tariff No. 1704.90.3550 (2003)—**Big Squirt Candy Spray**—Hungary—0.81 ounces of liquid candy syrup. . . . Consume the candy syrup by spraying it directly into the mouth. Strawberry, green apple and blue raspberry flavors. Strawberry sample submitted is bright pink fluid. Harmonized Tariff Schedule of United States (HTS); entitled to duty free treatment under Generalized System of Preferences (GSP).*

*Tariff No. 1704.90.3550; 1806.32.3000 (2000)—**A Foot of Fudge, A Yard of Chocolate**—England—Yard of Chocolate 36 inches long, two inches wide. Harmonized*

Tariff Schedule of United States (HTS). Does not comply with Section 304 of Tariff Act of 1930 as amended (19 U.S.C. 1304).

*Tariff No. 1704.10.0000; 1704.90.3550 (2006)—**Smarties, X-Treme Sour Smarties, Tropical Smarties, Smarties Candy Money Rolls, Smarties Bubble Gum**—Canada—Harmonized Tariff Schedule of United States (HTS). Under facts provided, X-Treme Sour Smarties, Tropical Smarties and Smarties Candy Money Rolls qualify for preferential treatment pursuant to General.*

Note 12(b), HTSUS (19 U.S.C. 1202). However, [are] subject to Public Health Security and Bioterrorism Preparedness and Response Act of 2002.

White as Snow

In Adams County, Colorado, all male massage parlor employees must wear all-white slacks and all-white shirts. No transparent clothing is permitted (Ordinance of the Board of County Commissions, Adams County, Colorado (1989)).

Tassel-Free

In 2005, a year early, King Mswati III of Swaziland ended a law requiring teenage girls to wear tassels in their hair as a sign of their chastity.

Even in a country in which 40 percent of the population was infected with HIV, the law was extremely unpopular, especially after the king himself had relations with a seventeen-year-old girl, a transgression for which he fined himself a cow.

At a sunrise ceremony commemorating the end of the law, thousands of the tassels were set on fire, then thirty thousand Swazi girls danced bare-breasted in a stadium before the leering king, who at the annual reed dance a few days later chose his thirteenth wife.

Pumping the Prime

In New Orleans, it is unlawful for any person to "inflate or blow" meat sold for human consumption (New Orleans Municipal Code, Health and Sanitation, § 82-53).

Indecent Exposure

High-minded authorities are now banning low-riding pants.

In 2008, Flint, Michigan's Chief Dick, railing against "immoral self-expression," began rounding up teens with loose pants and presumably the morals to match; by the end of the year, eleven behinds had been pinched by police for indecent exposure and disorderly conduct.

Exposing some underwear but no skin is a Class C offense and will result in a warning. A sag below the glutteal curve but that exposes only the underwear is a Class B offense. Any sagging leading to exposure of rear cleavage is a Class A offense. Penalties range from fines to ninety-three days in jail. Meanwhile, the 2007 *Congressional Quarterly* ranked Flint the third most dangerous city in America.

In 2008, the Hahira, Georgia, City Council passed a similar ordinance; at the same meeting the council discussed a law restricting ownership of snakes, bears, and wildcats and approved an application to sell beer at the Bigfoot Travel Center on Highway 122W.

Mayor Broussard of Delcambre, Lousiana, shrugged off accusations of racial profiling when she banned low-riding, claiming that white people wear saggy pants, too, but Little Rock, Arkansas, decided to back away from an ordinance banning the pants as well as backward baseball caps after a dressing down by the American Civil Liberties Union.

The Jackson, Mississippi, City Council in 2009 considered a saggy pants ban sponsored by a councilman determined to "save all the children we can," but the ordinance was rejected by fellow members concerned with legal exposure. Mayor Melton announced his intention to override the veto. "I certainly respect the Constitution, but we have some issues that are much bigger."

Sushi Samarai

After convening an advisory panel of food luminaries and intellectuals in 2006, the Japanese Ministry of Culture began dispatching sushi squads to major cities of the world to inspect sushi restaurants for authenticity and adherence to traditional Japanese cooking techniques and standards. A summer trial run dispatched inspectors to eighty Japanese restaurants in Paris and other sushi squads scoured the planet, seeking to purge the culinary world of such sushi sacrilege as tempura-battered onion rings, Philadelphia rolls, and avocado anything.

The Upper Crust

After a ten-year battle, the Melton Mowbray Pork Pie Association proudly announced in 2008 the securing of Protected Geographical Indication status for its pig-filled protégé, pursuant to European Union Council Regulation (EEC) No 2081/92.

The EU passed laws in 1992 protecting brands and production methods deemed unique to certain regions. Roquefort cheese, for example, can be produced only from ewes grazing in a small sliver of the Larzac Plain and aged by a certain fungus unique to natural caves found in the Aveyron area of France.

The pampered pie didn't achieve its exalted status easily—it was engaged in multiple lawsuits for years with peeved pie bakers outside of Melton Mowbray. But the pie's perseverance did receive continuing admiration from the Pork Pie Appreciation Society of Ripponden, which meets every Saturday.

Mowbray's finest, which according to the association must have a gray inside and a limp, soggy exterior, now teams with rough-and-tumble cousin the Arbroath Smokie to join such effete French delicacies as *Beaurre des Deax Sevres*, *Agneau du Quercy*, and *Crottin de Chavignol*.

Even among such luxe dining companions, the struggle to keep atop the food pyramid is a brutal one, and the Mowbray Pork Pie may soon have competition from its archrival, the Cornish Pasty Association. Pasty promoters from Cornish country, though riven by internal dissension over carrots in the filling, have nonetheless united to apply for their own protected status, and in 2000, South West Liberal Democrat MEP Graham Watson presented a Cornish Pasty to European Union Food Commissioner Dr. Franz Fischler at EU headquarters in Brussels. Nine years later, the application is still under consideration.

Meanwhile, Cumberland Sausage recently received official backing from the highest echelons of British government and is about to make its own application.

6

Entertainment and Leisure

There is something in a bureaucrat that
does not love a poem.
—Gore Vidal, American novelist and essayist

L ife is hard, and that we occasionally seek pleasure and sometimes even meaning in our few spare moments seems particularly irksome to some; whether we act out a drama, ride a bicycle, or thrill to an acrobat walking a tightrope, our government does its bureaucratic best to get in on the act. Restless officials regulate the pillows we sleep on, how we blow up balloons, and even what we sing, as illustrated in the laws and statutes highlighted here.

Fancy Riding

460. Coasting Forbidden to Bicyclists. No bicycle shall be allowed to proceed in any street of the city by inertia or momentum, with the feet of the rider removed from the pedals.

461. Trick Riding Forbidden. No rider of a bicycle shall remove both hands from the handle-bars, or practice any trick or fancy riding in any street (Code of Ordinances of the City of New York (1906); since repealed).

The Master of the Revels

The lights dimmed on London's Broadway in the late 1500s, as earnest government officials sought to deter boisterous crowds and rampant frivolity.

In 1580, the lord mayor wrote a letter to the lord chancellor claiming that "great disorder had been committed at the Theatre on Sunday last," and advising him that the players of plays and tumblers and such were a superfluous sort of men and a hindrance to the service of God. He further said that these men and their wicked and unchaste manners were a great corrupter of youth and the occasion of much incontinence, frays, and quarrels and requested an order shutting down plays and theaters.

The request was apparently granted, because in a 1581 letter the lord mayor was instructed to reopen the theaters, to give the struggling players some work, and to allow them to "rehearse for the solace of Her Highness this next Christmas." The righteous lord mayor replied that afternoon hearers were watching rehearsals instead of attending church and that crowds might worsen the spread of the plague, and thus requested that the ban continue or at the least that a grave and discreet person be appointed to supervise.

The lord mayor was proven right years later; in 1592, the Court of Alderman said youths of the city were being corrupted by the theaters, at which resided "the light and the lewd, and harlots, cutpurses, cozeners and pilferers, all of whom devised evil and ungodly conspiracies and confederacies."

Parade of Horrors

Mardi Gras isn't much fun. Pursuant to the Prohibited Throws law, no Mardi Gras parade participant along the route can possess any "life-threatening objects," including "bomb bags," noxious substances, plastic spears, insects, marine life and rodents (dead or alive), condoms, or corrugated boxes (Code of Ordinances, City of New Orleans, § 34-28).

Not So Scary

In Topeka, Kansas, haunted houses must be on zoned C-4 commercial property, and it's against the law for frightened visitors to be disorderly or cause a disturbance.

Domino Theory

In Alabama, neither dice nor cards can be played in a poolroom. But dominoes may be played in a poolroom without fine or penalty in counties having more than

56,500 but less than 59,000 people, as determined by the 1970 or any subsequent federal decennial census (Code of Alabama, § 34-6-12).

Since, according to the latest U.S. Census Bureau decennial census in 2000, no Alabama county had a population between 56,500 and 59,000 people, no Alabama residents at present may play dominoes in a poolroom pursuant to the law, at least until the next decennial census is officially published.

Residents of Alabama's Blount County appear to be the most likely to be able to play dominoes in a poolroom without fine or penalty in the future, since the U.S. Census Bureau's 2008 estimated population for the county is 57,441, well within the legally mandated population range.

Down in Front

In Columbus, Georgia, "it shall be unlawful to wear a hat or any other covering of the head which obstructs the view of other persons in any theater" (Columbus, Georgia Municipal Code, § 14-28).

Deflated

Balloons are being burst in many jurisdictions.

Florida bans the release by a person, firm, or corporation of more than ten lighter-than-air balloons within a twenty-four-hour period (Florida Statutes, Ch. 372.995), while Virginia prohibits the release of fifty or more balloons within one hour and sets fines at $5 per balloon beyond the allowable limit (Code of Virginia, § 29). But in several other states balloon busters' hopes have been deflated, as anti-balloon legislation has been vetoed.

The statutes arise from concerns over marine life, which, some scientists claim, eat and sometimes die from a balloon's rubbery remains, which they say degrades slowly and is often mistaken for jellyfish and eaten. Balloon boosters claim that balloons fragment in midair and then degrade harmlessly.

California has joined the party poopers—its Penal Code 653 outlaws the release of foil- and Mylar-type balloons in large groups and requires sellers to affix a counterweight so they can't fly. The law was sponsored by California utilities, who say balloons land on power lines and cause dozens of outages a year, although this claim is vigorously denied by the Balloon Council.

California senator Jack Scott in 2008 proposed legislation that bans toys and candy from being tied to balloons, fearful that the balloons will become airborne because children will remove the toys and eat the candy.

Pay to Play

In Finland, a 2002 ruling by the country's highest court ordered that taxi drivers who play music while driving passengers must pay royalties to composers and recording artists.

Teosto, the Finnish copyright society, sued taxi driver

Lauri Luotonen, claiming that his passengers benefited from the music just as much as customers in cafes or restaurants, which also pay royalties. The court agreed, and ordered Luotonen to pay €22 annually.

Still Dry

Florida cops who bust a liquor still don't get to party much afterward. In the case of seizure of any large and immovable "still, doubler, worm, worm tub . . . or . . . any mash, wort or wash," the seizing officers are allowed to confiscate not more than one pint of booze for use as evidence (Florida Statutes, Alcoholic Beverages and Tobacco, Ch. 562.42).

Spot On

Spotters spend their spare time ogling buses, trains, and planes. Mostly a British pastime, a leading bus-spotting website endeavors to explain the hobby's mysterious attraction—aside from just memorizing bus schedules, it exults, spotting also involves collecting bus memorabilia, collating routes, and obtaining relevant bus literature. Highly recommended is Buses on Screen, a website celebrating breakout roles for busses in film, with Sandra Bullock's *Speed* considered a cinematic high-water mark.

For years, spotting was considered an eccentric but harmless pastime, no more threatening than stamp collecting. But recently, the British government has declared spotters to be nuisances, criminals, or worse, and hobbyists now find themselves the objects being watched, photographed, and identified.

Rob McCaffrey of Gloucestershire, married and respectably employed, compiled a collection of thirty thousand bus and tram photographs. In 2008, he was pinched by Pontypridd police pursuant to England's Prevention of Terrorism Act of 2000 (§ 44) and the Police and Criminal Evidence Act (PACE) of 1984, and then arrested again a few months later. Now he stays home.

With nearly 160,000 Rob McCaffreys having been stopped at British train stations alone, spotters were electrified when in 2009 Liberal Democrat MP Norman Baker gave a rousing defense of their eccentric hobby. "Trainspotting may be an activity of limited and indeed questionable appeal," he said stirringly, "but it is not a criminal offence."

Also not a criminal offense was the photo taking of Duane Kerzic, who in 2008 took photos of Amtrak trains from the platform of New York's Penn Station. Kerzic was handcuffed to a wall by two Amtrak police and an explosive-sniffing dog but eventually released on a technicality—he was taking photos for Amtrak's annual "Picture Our Train" calendar photo contest.

Kryptonite

Even Superman can't get past the Canadian border; he, and all crime-fighting superheroes, have been banned from the country since 1949. As per today's Canadian Criminal Code:

(1) Every one commits an offence who . . .

(b) Makes, prints, publishes, distributes, sells or has in his possession for the purpose of publication, distribution or circulation a crime comic.

DEFINITION OF "CRIME COMIC"

(7) In this section, "crime comic" means a magazine, periodical or book that exclusively or substantially comprises matter depicting pictorially

(a) The commission of crimes, real or fictitious; or

(b) events connected with the commission of crimes, real or fictitious, whether occurring before or after the commission of the crime (Canada Criminal Code, § 163).

Gift That Keeps Giving

In Massachusetts, a gift certificate must be good for at least seven years (Ch. 510 of Acts of 2002; Ch. 18, Acts of 2003).

Bowling

For seven hundred years bowling and bowling alleys have been deemed dangerous and contrary to the public welfare by government officials.

Bowling's image problem began in the Middle Ages,

when English alleys supposedly became a haven for gambling, unlawful assembly, and idling in general.

In 1366, a statute was signed that barred citizens from bowling so they could spend more time practicing archery. A 1541 statute, the Bill for Maintaining Artillery and the Debarring of Unlawful Games, banned bowling and other crafty games like Logetting in the Fields and Slidethrift, also known as Shove-groat.

In 1580, the lord mayor of London stopped the building of Sir James Croft's indoor bowling alley, writing that the alley would attract only the worst and meanest persons, who would gamble and play while their families starved.

A letter from the Lords of the council to the lord mayor in 1583 bemoaned laxity in the enforcing of laws against unlawful games like bowling, noting disorder and lewd and evil expenses as well as the decline of the archery industry. The reply letter agreed, finding that these unlawful games, and spectacles like bearbaiting, caused unchaste interludes and bargains of incontinence, which would only draw God's wrath upon the city.

Years later, a letter from the longbow makers said that bowling alleys were putting them out of business, and by 1627 they desperately petitioned the Lords for relief: "The mystery of making Longbows is likely to be utterly forgotten in this kingdom." Later that year the Lords sponsored an archery competition, awarding 20 shillings to the victor.

Meanwhile, in the Virginia of 1610, Sir Thomas Dale arrived to take command and found settlers dying of starvation but bowling in the streets; he immediately drew up the draconian Laws Divine, which sent bowlers to the pillory.

In nineteenth-century United States, various laws were passed banning bowling for the usual reasons—gambling, drinking, and related vices—and in the 1930s, bowling is said to have been prohibited in some areas of the South because employees were missing too much work.

Today, most jurisdictions require permits and elaborate safety precautions just to own and even paint bowling alleys. Typical is Boston, which strictly regulates lane finishing and mandates that pin refinishing be done in a special room (Fire Prevention Code, Art. IV, § 4.04). In Wayne, Nebraska, pin refinishing is prohibited altogether (BRC 717.08).

Taking up where English kings left off, there are now no bowling "alleys" in Lincoln, Nebraska, where an ordinance was introduced changing the name to the more wholesome *lanes* (§ 5.14.050), which are now located in "Public Bowling Centers" instead of tawdry bowling alleys (§ 5.14.060).

Fake Wrestling?

In Louisiana, anyone who conducts a sham wrestling exhibition shall forfeit his license to stage similar exhibitions in the future (Louisiana Code, RS-4:75).

Glow Stick

In 2001, the American Civil Liberties Union defended the right to wear glow sticks and dance heedlessly with our hands in the air.

Owners of a prominent New Orleans rave venue were charged with promoting sales of Ecstasy and faced a sentence of twenty-five years, but frustrated feds couldn't make a case, and settled on a plea that merely banned glow sticks, pacifiers, surgical masks, and other "drug paraphernalia."

The ACLU moved for an injunction, claiming the plea bargain violated partygoers' free speech and search and seizure rights.

At the hearing, the U.S. attorney claimed that glow sticks were rubbed over the eyes and surgical masks smeared with Vicks VapoRub, both to enhance Ecstasy's sensory appeal. ACLU lawyers presented a college professor, who testified that glow sticks and baby pacifiers weren't drug paraphernalia at all, and partiers, whose rights were infringed by the ban, including an ex-member of the Air Force Sabre Drill Team, who had practiced dance routines for his Air Force unit, and an insurance salesman, who attended raves in a Mr. Bunny costume and handed out candy.

The plea bargain was deemed unconstitutional and squelched by a permanent injunction.

Web Surfing Safari

In rare agreement, animal lovers and hunters united to condemn a game farm promoting Internet hunting, where remote "shooters" used webcams and a joystick to trigger a rifle that shot animals passing within range.

Until the operation was shut down, a monthly subscription of $14.95 and $150 an hour entitled a person at a computer screen a thousand miles away to aim and "shoot" a mounted rifle, with options of having the meat from the kill frozen and shipped and the hide stuffed by a taxidermist.

Most customers appeared to subscribe because they were too scared or lazy to actually venture outdoors, but Dale Hagberg saw things a little differently. A former hunter and now a quadriplegic who breathes through a tube, he said, "I'm sure when I see the animal walk in my view, my heart will start beating as fast as it used to." During his four sessions, Hagberg chose not to pull the trigger. "Its not about killing them," he said. "[I]f they [critics] walked in my shoes for a while . . . they'd feel differently."

At least thirty-five states now ban Internet hunting, but many accommodate disabled hunters with mechanical assistance. In Wisconsin, disabled hunters can hunt from vehicles (§ 29.103, for example), and wheelchair-mounted rifles designed for high-level quads are now widely distributed. In Vermont, legislators permit the disabled to use semiremote hunting technology, allowing the use of remote control to see and shoot as long as the device is in the immediate vicinity and not Internet controlled (Ch. 113, § 4715).

And the Band Played On . . .

In Michigan, it is illegal to play the national anthem in public as part of a medley of songs, even patriotic ones, and the anthem must be played all the way through. The penalty ranges up to ninety days imprisonment (Michigan Compiled Laws, 750.542, Penal Code Act 328 (1948)).

Turning the Tables

Chefs simmering over the latest bad review may do better wielding a frying pan than suing for libel.

American libel law is particularly stringent pursuant to *New York Times Co. v. Sullivan*, 376 U.S. 254 (1964), where the Supreme Court held that to prevail in a libel suit the plaintiff had to prove not just bogus facts but also "actual malice," meaning knowingly publishing a falsehood or recklessly failing to investigate.

Steamed chefs still sue, usually in cases involving more fact than opinion. In 2006, a critic complained that a meal at Delmonico's Grill in Port St. Lucie, Florida, was not fresh, but the chef claimed his receipts showed purchase of the ingredients just two hours before serving the food. A lawsuit by Il Romano in Dallas against a local newspaper settled with both sides agreeing to a second review, after the 1994 original found a tomato vodka sauce "overwrought" with butter and ravioli soaked with gorgonzola sauce, ingredients the chef claimed weren't even used.

The owner of upscale Chops in Philadelphia is suing critic Craig LeBan, winner of the prestigious James Beard award, over a blurb finding his strip steak miserably tough and fatty. LeBan, who reviews anonymously, appeared at a videotaped deposition wearing a wig and fake beard, but was ordered by the judge to take them off. England's widely respected critic A. A. Gill has yet to be sued, despite having written a review of a London restaurant that began, "Why is there never a Palestinian suicide bomber when you need one?"

Answered Prayers

God and religion finally won the big one in 2009, as church-backed legislation brought the powerful National Football League to its knees.

Until 2009, the league banned churches from having Super Bowl parties using televisions larger than fifty-five inches, claiming copyright infringement. Church groups protested, claiming they showed the game not for profit but for charity and to increase interest among the young. The Christian Coalition and leaders like Reverend David Greene invoked Matthew 29:18–20 and declared that, to see the Super Bowl, "God's people have to take a stand."

A stand was taken by powerful Senators Orrin Hatch and Arlen Specter, who in 2008 sponsored Senate Bill S259, which provided non-profit organizations an exemption from this type of copyright infringement claim. The league capitulated, and now church groups can watch The Game with religious zeal.

Party Poopers

TERRIBONE PARISH LAWS, LOUISIANA, § 19-12

SILLY STRING SALES RESTRICTIONS:
(b) It shall be illegal for any persons to sell any silly string, or its equivalent, as defined herein . . . on any day a parade is scheduled.

It's the Same Old Song

In *Bright Tunes Music v. Harrisongs Music*, one of the world's most gifted and original songwriters was sued for copying someone else's song.

In 1962, "He's So Fine" was written by Ronald Mack and produced by the Tokens ("The Lion Sleeps Tonight"). Years later, a young musician named George Harrison composed the haunting "My Sweet Lord," which first became a number one hit, then the target of a plagiarism lawsuit.

At trial, Harrison conceded that he had heard "He's So Fine" at least once before but insisted that the contested melody was entirely his own. But even Harrison's own music composition expert found that "My Sweet Lord" and "He's So Fine" had in common an unusual repetition of key musical phrasing, especially in the *sol-mi-re*, *sol-la-do-la-do*, and *sol-la-do-la-re-do* sequences, and Harrison himself agreed that the songs were substantially similar.

The court ruled for the plaintiff, finding that the two songs were virtually identical, but the decision, footnoted with notes and chords, made a point of absolving Harrison of any conscious intent to copy. An appeal ensued, but an appellate court ruled that Harrison's innocent state of mind was no bar to the liability finding against him.

Bouncy Castles

Pursuant to a landmark 2008 English tort decision, operators of Bouncy Castles will no longer be held liable for failing to exercise continuous supervision over children.

Elaborate, jumbo-size air mattresses on which children jump and tumble, Bouncy Castles are often rented by English parents to celebrate birthdays and the like. In this case, young boys were doing somersaults while the supervising mother was tending to another child with her back turned. The injured boy was accidentally kicked in the head by another, much larger boy, and suffered permanent brain damage.

Conservative commentators hailed the ruling, saying accidents will happen, while the boy's parents pointed to prior similar incidents and warnings given by the industry itself telling parents not to mix big kids with small (*Harris v. Perry*, EWCA, Civ 907, British Court of Appeals (2008)).

For Sale

Pursuant to a Georgia law still in effect:

> *Any person who shall sell, apprentice, give away, let out, or otherwise dispose of any minor under twelve years of age to any person for the vocation, occupation, or service of rope or wire walking, begging, or as a gymnast, contortionist, circus rider, acrobat, or clown . . . shall be guilty of a misdemeanor (Georgia Code, 39-2-17).*

At Odds

Legal poker is a good bet but not a sure thing. Online, the Unlawful Internet Gambling Enforcement Act (2006) makes it illegal for banks and credit card companies to transfer money to poker websites, and the FBI's website warns against playing. But even the website's own slogan, "Online Gambling, Don't Roll the Dice," reveals the bluff, and no one yet has been prosecuted. Several bills to legalize and regulate online gambling and poker are now pending.

Decisions around the country go both ways, sometimes in the same case. When poker players were recently raided by a SWAT team in full battle gear, a South Carolina judge ruled Texas Hold'em to be a game of skill but reluctantly found the defendants guilty of running a gambling house.

Submitted in the case was a Friends of the Court brief from the Poker Players Alliance, which noted that quantum mechanics pioneer John von Neumann included an entire chapter about poker in one of his seminal mathematics books, and also discussed the finer points of tells and bluffing (*Town of Mt. Pleasant v. Robert L. Chimento et al., Charleston County* (2009)).

Decisions in Pennsylvania are also split. "If you did a survey of the 67 district attorneys in Pennsylvania, you would probably get 67 different opinions on what constitutes illegal gambling in terms of poker," said a spokesman from the Pennsylvania attorney general's office.

I'm the Director, the Monster's over There

Englishwoman Julie Burchill is one tough critic. In the *London Sunday Times* she reviewed *The Age of Innocence*. But her review of the movie didn't bother well-known actor and director Steven Berkoff—what really hurt was Burchill's description of him as "hideous looking."

Just months later, Burchill reviewed Berkoff's *Frankenstein* and repeated the slur, comparing the looks of the monster to its director, and Berkoff again came up short. A court refused to dismiss Berkoff's defamation case, holding that based on Burchill's statements reasonable jurors could read the reviews and find that Berkoff was indeed repulsive (*Berkoff v. Burchill* (1996)).

Hands On

Pursuant to the Illinois vehicle code, a person operating a bicycle shall keep one hand on the handlebars at all times (Illinois Vehicle Code § 11-1506).

A Perfect 10

In 2009, a lawmaker aligned with France's dominant political party introduced a bill to the National Assembly requiring warning labels and disclaimers on digitally retouched and "misleading" images of people in magazine ads and articles. The bill was designed primarily to combat anorexia and feelings of inferiority among impressionable young women striving for fashion-induced perfection, although the proposed $55,000 fine could have also applied to a widely published photo featuring France's president Nicolas Sarkozy shirtless, with his bulging waistline artfully airbrushed out of existence.

In 2008, the same National Assembly passed a bill making it illegal for any person or entity, including fashion magazines, advertisers, and websites, to incite extreme thinness, with fines of up to $71,000 and three-year prison sentences, but the legislation didn't make it through the French Senate.

That bill followed on the heels of a 2006 Madrid City Council bill that did go into effect, banning ultra-skinny women from appearing in fashion shows. Models with body-mass indexes of less than eighteen are now prohibited from the catwalk, with medics on standby to inspect the merchandise and enforce the edict.

No Dice

In Massachusetts, a person who gambles within twelve hours and one mile of a cattle show, military muster, or public gathering can be arrested without warrant. A person caught in the act can be held in jail for twenty-four hours, except on Sundays (Massachusetts General Laws, Ch. 271, 6).

Three-Ring Circus

English circuses are juggling to comply with recent changes in the law.

In 2008, the UK Border Agency began implementing its new points-based system, designed to exercise more selectivity over immigration applicants to the country. Circus performers, like clowns and acrobats, easily met the skilled worker requirements, but were held back by technicalities and bureaucratic bungling; ringmaster Martin Lacey had a clown stuck in Mexico, acrobats stranded in Ukraine, and horse riders without visas in Ulan Bator.

Given the Brits' notoriously dry sense of humor, talented homegrown clowns are few and far between; when questioned before Parliament as to why there weren't any

"British clowns for British circuses," a circus official testified that there is simply no demand for native British clowns, ever.

British circuses have also struggled with recent European Union regulations that apparently require acrobats and trapeze artists to wear hard hats. EU leader Jose Manuel Barroso pointedly denied the existence of such laws in a recent speech, but after consultation with EU officials, a consortium of seven insurance companies faxed the Moscow State Circus UK an advisory notice requiring its acrobats and tightrope walkers to wear safety headgear based on EU regulations. Tightrope walker Goussein Khamdouleav, who while performing wears a fur Cossack hat, not a helmet, was dismissive, and the circus general manager said, "This is just another loony law from Brussels (home of the European Union) and we are the only country stupid enough to pay attention."

On the Ball

Utah bureaucrats are ready for that moment we all fear, when our car is hit and damaged by an errant golf ball from a county golf course.

After a car is struck and a claim filed, a comprehensive investigation is undertaken and a formal report issued. The report is then forwarded to the district attorney for determination. If deemed appropriate, monies are disbursed by a risk manager from a dedicated golf ball damage fund, subject to further rules and regulations propagated by the risk manager.

An application can be denied if not timely submitted or if the damage was caused by an irresponsible act of the applicant or an agent or a member of the applicant's business or household. A reduction of payment in golf ball damage can result if the loss exceeds the funding limits of the statute, if verification of the loss was inadequate, or if the applicant did not act responsibly to minimize the loss (No-Fault Golf Ball Claims Ordinance, Health and Recreation, 13.24.010-090).

Fore!

In Massachusetts, anyone who manufactures, sells, or possesses an explosive golf ball faces imprisonment for a term of not more than one year (General Laws, Ch. 148, § 55).

Feet, Tails, and Brains

Spam maker Hormel became Oscar the Grouch when the Muppets used a piggish character named Spa'am to star in its *Muppet Treasure Island* movie.

Hormel claimed that the movie's depiction of Spa'am as "evil in porcine form" infringed upon its trademark and would interfere with sales of Spam Classic, Spam Hot & Spicy, and Spam Spread ("if you're a spreader, not a slicer"), and also impugn the brand's reputation.

Relying on a children's literature expert, the lower court ruled against Hormel on the infringement claim, finding that Spa'am, high priest of a tribe of boars that worshiped Miss Piggy, was, although not "classically handsome," an essentially positive figure, especially because he helped Miss Piggy, Fozzie Bear, and Kermit the Frog escape villainous Long John Silver.

In regard to "reputation," the court noted in its opinion that Spam's reputation had not quite reached the heights the company had claimed for it, citing a recent newspaper column from the *Orlando Sentinel* saying that Spam contained "The five major food groups: Snouts, Ears, Feet, Tails & Brains" (*Hormel Foods Corporation v. Jim Henson Productions Inc.*, U.S. Ct. Appeals, Second Circuit (1996)).

Tough Audience

At a sporting exhibition in Louisiana, there shall be no insulting or abusive remarks directed at participants, no matter how badly they play (Louisiana Code, Title 4, RS 4:81).

Corrupt Stuffings

Alert government officials have been supervising how we sleep for over five hundred years. Lawmakers of the Middle Ages started the trend around 1485, with Henry VII issuing a royal proclamation:

> *Each featherbed, bolster or pillow for sale shall be stuffed with one type of stuffing, that is, dry-pulled feathers, or*

with clean down alone, and with no sealed feathers nor marsh grass, nor any other corrupt stuffings. Each quilt, mattress or cushion for sale shall be stuffed with one type of stuffing . . . and with no horsehair, marshgrass, neats-hair, dearshair or goatshair, which is wrought in lime-fats and gives off an abominable and contagious odor when heated by a man's body.

In Delaware, the tagging of all bed articles except a feather- or down-filled pillow, bolster, bed, or comforter is required, and the state outlaws the use of the words *curled hair* if other than curled hair is used in the filling of mattresses, pillows, bolsters, or comforters (Delaware Title 16, Health and Safety, Ch. 2).

Ontario allows the sale of pillows and mattresses that contain vermin as long as they've been sterilized or disinfected but does require plumage cleanliness (Ontario Regulation 218/01 (2008)).

Manly Texas takes a firm approach to mattresses, with its ominous Bedding Rule Critical Violation of Severity Level III netting a fine of up to $10,000 a day and multiple violations costing up to $25,000 daily. In Texas, a tag in a recliner chair must be attached to the underside of the footrest and nowhere else (Texas Administrative Code, Title 25, Part 1, Ch. 205, Subchap. A, Rule 205.4). The state goes soft on plumules, which are required only to be downy waterfowl plumage with underdeveloped soft and flaccid quills, although the quills must have barbs, and the word *feathers* by itself should not be used. While emu feathers are allowed, the words *comber*, *noils*, and *picker motes* can be used only under certain exceptional circumstances (Rule 205.5). The presence of a metal spring in a mattress must be listed last, but stating the number of coils is not required (Rule 205.3).

Our comfort is guaranteed in Winona County, Minnesota, where as of 2009 all hotels and resorts must provide unworn blankets, pillows, and mattresses (Sec. IV, 13.7). In group homes in Ohio, any individual needing to sleep in a crib shall sleep in one at least six inches longer than his or her extended length (Ohio Administrative Code 5123.2, Ch. 5123:2-3-10(f)).

7

People Getting Along

Our most important laws concern how we treat each other. Some are life and death, most aren't, and many address our everyday bump and grind against people having the same weaknesses, hungers, and occasional desire to take advantage as we do. The laws here, current or from the recent past, govern conduct with which we may be somewhat unacquainted, from being a scold to dueling to being ugly in public:

Rixitrix

From the Middle Ages until at least the 1970s, women (only) perceived to be difficult were prosecuted for being communis rixitrix—that is, common scolds.

Beginning in the 1600s, England and then colonial

America's cure for the common scold was the ducking stool, an armchair attached to the end of a long beam used to dunk the victim in the water. Sometimes the apparatus was mounted on wheels to parade the victim about town; alternative devices included the brank, a metal face mask with spikes that pricked an active tongue, and a dung chair, designed to expose the buttocks. The last recorded ducking was probably that of Sarah Leeke of England in 1817, but in New Jersey in 1972 Marion Palendrano was arrested for assault and for being a scold pursuant to N.J.S.A. 2A:85-1, the court defining "A Common Scold" as being "a troublesome and angry woman . . . a nuisance to the neighborhood"; the charge was later struck down by a higher court (*State v. Palendrano*, 120 N.J. Super 336 (1972)).

Over the years, many scolds, shrews, and strumpets in the Northeast were vigorously prosecuted, often to the glee of vengeful neighbors. Barbara Fritchy was indicted for hallooing a nearby family, and foulmouthed Mary Monoghan insisting she was framed by neighbors. "It's a put-up job by someone who wants to get square," claimed her equally tough-talking husband. In 1893, Elizabeth Schultze of Hoboken, New Jersey, was convicted of inter- esting herself in everyone's business, and a woman in Chautauqua County, New York, paid a fine for her torrent of words, and not the choicest kind, either.

In 1889, Mary Braden was tried in Jersey City, New Jersey; prosecutors insisted that only the scold statute could measure the length of her tongue. Winifred Doody testified that Braden often called her a gray-haired hag, but Braden's husband defended her, claiming she became abusive only when he stayed out late with the boys. An all-male jury convicted her in four minutes.

Indicted scold Frances McCarthy of Schuylerville, New York, was romantically linked with wealthy D. A. Bullard and used to go to Bullard's home to taunt his wife. She had the middle finger of her hand bitten half off but was acquitted of scolding by a jury. Her luck ran out in 1892 when she shot a disapproving hotel clerk in the jaw; a month later, McCarthy and the hotel clerk died within an hour of each other, both of blood poisoning.

In Pittsburgh, Pennsylvania, Mrs. Bridget Ruppie of Miflin Way was convicted of having the most voluminous vocabulary of epithets in the whole county and forced to move out of town, while Julia Green of White Plains, New York, was released from the Kings County Penitentiary after promising the judge not to boss around the entire neighborhood.

No Legitimate Purpose

It is now illegal to be annoying in the city of Brighton, Michigan.

Passed in December of 2008, Brighton's new law states "it shall be unlawful for a person to engage in a course of conduct or repeatedly commit acts that alarm or seriously annoy another person and that serve no legitimate purpose" (City of Brighton Code of Ordinances, Ch. 54, Art. IV, § 54-98 (c)).

Concerned about the law's potential for abuse, activist

Pat Cole was quoted in a meeting as saying that his mere presence could be annoying.

Basta, Basta

During Italy's 2008 "security emergency," mayors were given unprecedented law-and-order powers.

In the resort town of Eraclea, Mayor Teso has banned the building of sand castles on the beach. Using a lawn-mower on the weekends is illegal in luxe Forte dei Marmi on the Tuscan coast, since it may disturb someone taking a nap, and in Alto Ridge and Gran Paradiso, a person hunting mushrooms or picking berries will be fined €113. Mobs of three or more are prohibited at night in the parks of Novara.

In Vicenza, Rodrigo Piccoli was fined €50 for laying in the park and reading a book, while in Viareggio a person will be nabbed for putting his or her feet up on a bench.

Noisy wooden sandals are now forbidden in Capri, as is wandering off beach grounds in a bikini.

Ghost Story

Strict legal protections now apply to "Stigmatized Property," particularly residences burdened with death or haunting.

California typically started the trend, with *Reed v. King* (1983), in which the court of appeals found a duty to disclose when a purchaser bought a house ten years after a woman and her four children had been murdered inside. In the leading New York case of *Stambovsky v. Ackley* (169 A.D.2d 254 (1991)), Ackley sold her suburban house "as is" to Stambovsky, who was unfamiliar with the house's reputation. The Stambovsky family discovered to their horror that the house was possessed by poltergeists and had been the subject of several articles concerning Sir George and other assorted spooks. "We were the victim of ectoplasmic fraud," exclaimed a terrified Stambovsky. The court substantially agreed, declining to find actual fraud but canceling the contract anyway.

Many states now have strict disclosure laws. Typical is California's Civil Code § 1710.2, which combined with other statutes requires sellers to disclose at the very least notorious or gruesome deaths occurring within three years of sale. Similar laws have been adopted worldwide.

From a business standpoint, pesky poltergeists are best dealt with by combining the spectral with the practical. Mary-Pope Handy, the author of *Haunted Real Estate: A Primer for Real Estate Agents*, suggests that legal issues might be avoided altogether by being polite but firm with the haunters. "Mrs. Smith, I know you loved this home. . . . But this is my home now. . . . You really should move on. . . . It would be best if you crossed over." Failing this, the San Diego Paranormal Research Project will team up with the broker to assist with the buying and selling of haunted houses. Their lengthy list of buyers features a broad variety of tastes; Melissa seeks only "nonviolent activity," Julia prefers "tumultuous histories," and Caitlin and Michael will pay up to $350,000 for a three-bed/two-bath but prefer a positive presence because they have children.

On the sell side, #1021 is recently renovated and features

a wraparound driveway and shadow people. In #1017, two "houseguests" share a twenty-one-hundred-square-foot Victorian with a trophy view. And #1007 is warm and inviting, zoned for commercial use, and has both orbs *and* ectoplasm. All owners wish to sell as soon as possible.

England's Most Unwanted

Her Majesty's Court Service, an executive agency of England's Ministry of Justice, maintains a list of "vexatious litigants," individuals said to bring lawsuits in such number and of such little merit that they abuse the legal system and prevent more legitimate litigants from having their day in court. Vexatious litigants are forbidden by a high court from issuing civil proceedings in any court in England and Wales without permission.

Here is a list of 2009 vexatious litigants published by Her Majesty's Court Service, dealings with whom readers wishing to stay out of court may wish to avoid:

- Leslie James Adams
- Zainab Duke Abiola
- Adoko Akena
- Anthony Alexander
- George Harvey Allan
- Theosophilus Vincent Allan
- Haider Ali
- Azad Amin
- Dorothy Mignon Arnold (aka Gracie)

- Krishan Kuman Arora (for a period of twelve years only)
- Jack Auburn (aka Herbert Morton)

Dueling

Kentucky is finally cracking down on its dueling problem. Zealous lawyers must take an oath to refrain from sword or gunplay, in or out of the courtroom:

> *I do solemnly swear . . . I . . . have not fought a duel with deadly weapons . . . nor have I sent or accepted a challenge to fight a duel, nor have I acted as a second (Constitution of Kentucky, § 228).*

The constitution similarly disqualifies any job seeker who's participated in a duel from holding a state office of honor or profit (§ 239). And more determined than ever to contain the threat, in 1998 Kentucky specifically required first responders and members of disaster and emergency response organizations to take the same anti-dueling oath (Kentucky Revised Statutes 39A.210).

But Kentucky's dueling problem continues to fester, from both within and without state borders. It is a member of various mutual aid pacts with neighboring states, with those states authorized to send emergency assistance personnel in times of crisis. A careful reading of the Emergency Management Assistance Compact as codified by

Kentucky Revised Statutes § 39A.950 as set forth in the *Congressional Research Service (CRS) Report for Congress* (2004), combined with the included *Declaration Procedures*, reveals that state officials during emergencies can "waive procedures and formalities otherwise required by the law."

Thus, during times of disaster, a rogue Kentucky official can repeal the anti-dueling law for Kentucky employees and thereby create a loophole that allows Kentucky workers to duel with disaster aid workers from neighboring states that themselves don't renounce dueling, all this at a time when teamwork, not the settling of old scores, is vital to citizen health and welfare.

Information Please

In Canada, it is illegal to render data meaningless. The penalty ranges up to life imprisonment (Canada Criminal Code, § 430).

Spiritual Union

British psychics are forming a union, dispirited over new European Union laws that put them in solidarity with such lumpen proletariat as car salesmen and refrigerator repairmen.

Until 2008, psychics took pride in being governed by

special and sometimes exotic laws like the Fraudulent Mediums Act 1951 and before that the Witchcraft Act of 1735. Under the drab Unfair Commercial Practices Directive, psychics and mediums are now subject to the same consumer protection laws as everybody else, and, as with a leaky gasket, customers need not prove a sinister scheme to file a complaint or get a refund, just simple incompetence.

Spooked psychics envision giving receipts for readings and having to book séance spirits in advance, and are now lobbying to raise from the dead prior laws that essentially immunized them from such earthly concerns as being right. Faith healer Carole McEntee-Taylor, founder of the Spiritual Workers Association (SWA), laments that predicting the future has been turned into a consumer product, and worst of all, "we will now have to prove we are genuine."

Membership in Taylor's new spiritual union provides decidedly down-to-earth benefits, including competitive insurance premiums, a glossy trade magazine, business links, and accounting advice. Also provided to members are a broad range of written disclaimer forms to give to prospective clients.

Heartbreak Hotel

A Canadian who obtains free food, drink, or a room at a hotel by falsely pretending to have baggage is presumed guilty of fraud (Canada Criminal Code, Sec. § 364).

Foot Fetish

Running trains on time is only one priority for England's Merseyrail, which has now turned its attention to "antisocial behavior." Rail enforcement officers are using high-tech head cams to record and prosecute sociopathic deviants who put their feet on the seat.

So far thousands of "incidents" have been prosecuted in the Magistrate's Court, like the one involving nineteen-year-old special-needs volunteer Kathleen Jennings, who admitted she put her flip-flops on the seat for a few seconds. She quickly apologized but was nailed by a uniformed officer using a miniature camera mounted on his hat.

Jennings was found innocent, and the railway was rebuked by angry court magistrates for wasting its time, but Merseyrail remains unrepentant. "We will not tolerate antisocial behavior."

The Rule of Thumb

According to ancient English law, a husband was welcome to beat his wife to keep her in line as long as it was done with a stick no thicker than his thumb. But this "rule" might be an example of how folklore creates its own reality, to the point that even judges and courts are fooled.

In the North Carolina case of *State v. Rhodes*, 61 N.C. 453 (1868), a jury found that a husband struck his wife "three licks with a switch about the size of one of his fingers (but not as large as a man's thumb)." After the jury's finding about the size of the stick, the judge confirmed that "the defendant had a right to whip his wife with a switch no larger than his thumb, and that . . . he was not guilty in law." The appeals court found "no error."

The rule is also cited in several other cases, in a law review article ("Right of Husband to Chastise Wife," 3 *Virginia Law Register* 239 (1917)), and in several modern books, treatises, and articles.

But where's the statute? The great seventeenth-century legal historian Sir William Blackstone notes that in times past a husband could give his wife "moderate correction," but makes no mention of the rule of thumb. Extensive research by lawyers, librarians, and feminists has yet to turn up anything definitive.

Ant Farm

In China, raising ants at home promised to pay returns of 60 percent a year . . . guaranteed!

Poor farmers, anxious to grab their rung of the free enterprise ladder, enrolled by the tens of thousands in a scheme promoted by celebrities and government officials and widely advertised on state-run television. Sponsored by a respected consumer products company, ants were to be grown at home to make liquor and aphrodisiacs, with the finished product bought back by the company for big profits.

Cardboard boxes came with a small window and a feeding hole. The ants were to be fed with a mixture of water and sugar or honey at precisely 9:00 a.m. and 4:00 p.m. each day, and every five days cake and egg yolk were to be added. The box had to be kept indoors and always tightly sealed. Every seventy-four days, the company would come by and pick up the box, check in hand.

Scheme promotor Wang Zhendong was executed in November 2008.

Rat Race

Pink-eyed picketers emerged victorious in *State of New Jersey v. Wayne DeAngelo*, 2009 WL 291169 (N.J. 2/5/2009), where the state's highest court supported the First Amendment right to free speech of a union's giant inflatable rats. The rubbery rodents are used at labor rallies and demonstrations, with some of the pack measuring up to thirty feet high.

The controversy began when picketing union members were told by police to deflate the union rat, Scabby. When they refused, police ticketed the union rep for violating Lawrence Township Land Use Ordinance Section 3(L)(2), which prohibited "balloon signs or other inflated signs (except grand opening signs)."

The conviction was reversed by the New Jersey Supreme Court, which found that the ordinance impermissibly granted free speech to some but not others, based on what the signs said.

Union rodents have long navigated a maze of legal challenges. In *Kentov v. Sheet Metal Workers Local 15*, 418 F.3d 1259 (Eleventh Cir. 2005), a union rat picketed a hospital and was found to be in violation of secondary boycott laws by picketing a neutral party to stop it from doing business with the union's real target. In another secondary boycotting case, a judge revealed that a so-called rat was actually just a gorilla with a rat's head attached, and found against the union (Laborers' Eastern Region Organizing Fund, NLRB No. 29-CC-1422, CP-CP-622 (2005)).

The Ugly Laws

[H]e shall not approach: a blind man, or a lame, or he that hath a flat nose . . . or crookbackt, or a dwarf, or that hath a blemish in his eye.

—Leviticus 21:18–20

Chicago in 1974 had an all-time peak of 970 murders, but its virile, ruggedly handsome police force could have clamped down on an equally heinous threat: ugly people. Under the law, those with cerebral palsy, pocked faces, or amputated limbs who dared show their face in public risked arrest and conviction just for existing:

No person who is diseased, maimed, mutilated or in any way deformed so as to be an unsightly or disgusting object or improper person [is] to be allowed in or out of the public ways or other public places in this city, or shall therein or thereon expose himself to public view, under a penalty of not less than one dollar nor more than fifty dollars for each offense.

Similar laws existed in several other American cities and were not repealed until the mid-1970s (Chicago Municipal Code § 36034; Columbus, Ohio General Offense Code

§ 2387.04; Omaha Nebraska Unsightly Beggar Ordinance; Nebraska Municipal Code of 1941, § 25).

Racing Stripes

A Philadelphia speeding law from 1722:

> [It] is not only a very indecent and unseemly practice but very dangerous Consequence to the Inhabitants especially the Children Severall having been thrown down much Hurt and Narowly escaped with their Lives. . . . Be it Enacted . . . that If any person . . . shall Ride and gallop on an Excessive Swift Pace he shall . . . Pay the Sume of five shillings . . . in Cases Such Person shall be a Negro . . . He shall be Whipt . . . not exceeding fifteen Stripes (Philadelphia City Council Ordinances (1722)).*

Downtown

In England, it is currently illegal to, in the vicinity of a city street, roll a cask, tub, hoop, or wheel along a sidewalk; hang clothes; discharge a stone or other missile; disturb someone by putting out their lamp; fly a kite; sled on snow; expose oneself; sing a profane ballad; sift lime; or beat or shake any carpet, rug, or mat, except door mats beaten or

*A Negro could avoid being striped if his owner chose to pay the fine.

shaken before eight o'clock in the morning (Town Police Clauses Act of 1847, Ch. 89).

Hung Out to Dry

She hangs out a beautiful line.

—Italian saying

A campaign protecting our Right to Dry has spawned legislation that now allows citizens to legally hang their clothes to dry on a line despite homeowner association rules banning the practice.

An estimated sixty million Americans belong to these associations; a typical rule reads "clothes-drying apparatus . . . shall be screened from view" and ultimately mandates eviction upon violation.

According to a 2001 Energy Consumption Survey taken by the federal government's Energy Information Administration, clothes dryers account for 6 percent of the electricity consumed by U.S. households, and one private study claims that the drying of a typical T-shirt over a lifetime pumps nine pounds of carbon dioxide into the atmosphere, contributing to global warming.

Laundry liberation began quietly in the 1980s but gained momentum years later when the owner of a country store in Vermont and websites like Project Laundry List and Let's Hang Out encouraged people to hang their clothes in public and engage in civil disobedience if necessary.

In a 1999 opinion piece, Froma Harrop of the *Providence (Rhode Island) Journal* wrote, "Forbidding sheets . . . to flap in the New England sunshine is akin to banning boiled lobsters or requiring New Hampshire town clerks to smile."

But some homeowners and developers wish to hold the line, concerned with eyesores and plunging property values. Richard Monson of the California Association of Homeowner's Associations says visible clotheslines can lower property values by 15 percent and that "modern homeowners don't like people's underwear in public."

Several states now have laws explicitly protecting those who prefer their clothes dried in the breeze; Vermont's Energy Act of 2009 reads:

> [N]o municipality, by ordinance, resolution or other enactment, shall prohibit or have the effect of prohibiting the initiation of solar collectors, clotheslines, or other energy devices based on renewable resources.

A Hard Rain . . .

In Helena, Montana, "no person shall place any lawn sprinkler so that the water from same shall be thrown upon any street or sidewalk to the annoyance of passersby" (Helena City Code, Ch. 5-9-2).

Mayhem

A 2007 Wisconsin case about mayhem reads like a slasher movie but illustrates how difficult laws are interpreted.

Shannon Quintana was hit on the forehead with a hammer by ex-husband, Leonard, who was charged with mayhem. The issue was whether Shannon's forehead qualified as an "other bodily member."

Under Wisconsin Statute § 940.21, derived from England's Act to Prevent Maiming and Wounding (1671), this meant: "Whoever, with intent to disable or disfigure another, cuts or mutilates the tongue, eye, ear, nose, lip, limb or other bodily member of another is guilty of a Class C felony."

Quintana's lawyer claimed that "other bodily member" in this context meant only body parts closely related to those named in the statute, not the forehead. In response, the state's supreme court tried to determine whether the named body parts could reasonably be lumped together in some logical group that didn't include the forehead, as the lawyer claimed was appropriate, but the body parts were found to be essentially random. Quintana's lawyer next argued that given this ambiguity, the scope of "other body members" should be strictly limited and thus exclude the forehead.

But the court said limiting the intent of the statute too much would lead to absurd results—for example, pouring acid on a person's leg, a "limb," would be a crime, but pouring acid on a person's face would not be criminal, since it wasn't specifically mentioned in the law. Or a person could tattoo an obscene symbol on his or her victim's forehead and go free but be imprisoned for tattooing the back of the victim's arm.

The court then analyzed the meaning of *member* by looking in two different dictionaries but found conflicting interpretations. It also noted that in 1722 John Woodburne and Arundel Coke disfigured the face of a man with a hedge bill and claimed they intended only to kill the man, not maim him. They lost.

Short of convincing legal precedent one way or the other, after fifty pages the court upheld the broader interpretation and sustained the charge (*State of Wisconsin v. Quintana*, 299 Wis. 2d 234 (2007)).

Whitewash

In 1912, the Saskatchewan, Canada, legislature passed An Act to Prevent the Employment of Female Labour in Certain Capacities:

> *No person shall . . . permit any white woman . . . to work in . . . any restaurant, laundry or other place of business . . . owned, kept or managed by any Japanese, Chinamen or other Oriental person.*

The act was promoted by unions and competing laundries, and several other Canadian provinces soon followed suit. Shortly after enactment, the law was "liberalized" by taking out *Japanese* and *Oriental* and leaving just the Chinese. When two businessmen challenged the statute and were arrested for hiring white women, the case went all the way to the Supreme Court of Canada, which upheld their conviction. The act was subsequently amended, but continued to address the employment of "white women," and remained in effect until 1969.

Canada's attempt to stem the "yellow tide" was preceded by legislation in the United States, including California's bluntly worded An Act to Protect White Labor Against Competition with Chinese Coolie Labor, and to Discourage the Immigration of the Chinese into the State of California (1862), which imposed a tax on each person "of the Mongolian race." And the 1917 Immigration Act (39 Stat. 874, § 3) created an "Asiatic Barred Zone" south of the 20th parallel of latitude north, west of the 160th meridian of longitude east from Greenwich, and north of the 10th parallel of latitude south.

Big-Ticket Item

In egalitarian Finland, the amount you pay on a speeding ticket is determined by how fast you're going and how much you make.

In 2002, Anjssi Vanjoki, director of Finnish telecommunication giant Nokia, was caught driving forty-seven miles (seventy-five kilometers) per hour in a thirty-one-mile-(fifty-kilometer-) per-hour zone. Based on an estimated yearly income of roughly €12 million ($14 million), he was ordered to pay a fine of €116,000 ($103,600), believed to be the largest speeding ticket ever.

After a recalculation of his income based on Nokia's plunging share price, Vanjoki's fine was ultimately slashed to roughly $5,000.

Pop a Wheelie

Brits protective of their privacy are down in the dumps over Wheelie Bins, the British term for those square plastic trash cans on wheels. The bins are being turned into an army of undercover spies, designed to make criminals out of regular people dumping their trash.

Since 2006, the bins have been fitted with high-tech electronic sensors that detect how much trash has been thrown out and by whom; the information is transmitted to a central database. Over five hundred thousand cans were bugged in 2006 alone, mostly in government-sponsored housing developments.

The bugging was initially done in secret or with officials asserting that the spyware was installed to "resolve ownership disputes" over the trash cans. But it's now apparent that the bugs are a prelude to laws limiting the amount and perhaps even type of trash each household can throw out, and surely other alleged infractions down the road.

Trash cans in England have been a focus of periodic law enforcement crackdowns. A bus driver and father of four was busted by a SWAT-like team of police for overfilling his can by four inches; he ended up with a five-year criminal record and was ordered to pay a surcharge for victims of violent crimes. In Nottingham, penalties can reach £5,000 ($7,500) for leaving a bin out the day after trash collection; overwrought officials claim it poses a danger to blind people and parents pushing children in baby carriages.

Wok on the Wild Side

Pursuant to a 2008 Shanghai law, pedestrians who jaywalk across city streets are photographed and then shamed by being displayed on television and in newspapers.

In 2006, Shanghai police requested that law-abiding citizens photograph perpetrators and then give the photos to them for distribution to the offenders' employers, who were to fine the employees or withhold their pay.

Fines for jaywalking range from ¥5 to ¥50 (about $.60 to $6). Police try to collect the fines on the spot, but pedestrians often refuse to pay, claiming that they don't have the money or are being singled out unfairly. During the 2006 crackdown, police said dealing with an uncooperative jaywalker usually took three to four officers fifteen minutes.

Tsk, Tsk

The modern equivalent of the common scold is England's ASBO, or Anti-Social Behaviour Order.

First introduced in 1998 under the Crime and Disorder Act, it was later strengthened by the Anti-Social Behaviour Act of 2003. The order seeks to eliminate all conduct, including speech, likely to cause another harassment, "alarm," or "distress." The law now applies to anyone over the age of twelve, but authorities from the prime minister on down have tried to institute baby ASBOs (BASBOs) for little children. All ASBO violations carry sentences of up to five years for adults and two years' detention for children.

Stuart Hunt of Mid Balcchraggan Cottage Drumndrochit, Invernessshire, received an ASBO notice from authorities arising from a dispute with neighbors over a speed bump, and Hunt is now banned from laughing and staring at people, holding rude conversations, and clapping his hands slowly. At a court hearing, neighbors successfully argued it wasn't what he did but the way he did it that mattered.

Leopold Wrobel was jailed for months for whistling the *Addams Family* theme each time he saw an elderly couple. Amy Beth Dallamura was given an ASBO for her multiple suicide attempts.

According to a 2005 report commissioned by the House of Commons, ASBO powers are increasingly abused by authorities. Examples in the study included a teen arrested for "congregating" for attending a boy's club lecture on antisocial behavior, a thirteen-year-old boy banned from using the word *grass*, a sixteen-year-old prohibited from wearing a golf glove, and an eighty-seven-year-old prohibited from being sarcastic to his neighbors.

In 2009, the conduct of two-year-old Lennon Poyser and that of his sisters, Megan, four, and, Olivia, five, was cited in an ASBO notice on police stationery that was hand-served on their mother. The terror troika was accused of verbally abusing neighbors and destroying the property of a childless couple living next door, with Lennon accused of kicking a soccer ball over the fence. The boy's mother conceded that her two-year-old kicked a ball over the fence but said it was a toy soccer ball made of plastic, and it blew back to him in the wind.

Live Free or Die

Good men must not obey the laws too well.

—Ralph Waldo Emerson, American writer and philosopher

New Hampshire license plates bear the phrase "Live Free or Die," but the state doesn't always live up to its motto.

George Maynard, Korean War veteran and printer, taped over the slogan on the license plate of his family car in 1974, saying "I refuse to be coerced by the State into advertising a slogan which I find morally, ethically, religiously and politically abhorrent." He paid a $25 fine, continued to obscure the motto, and was jailed; the case ended up before the U.S. Supreme Court.

By a 6-3 decision the court held that a law that required Maynard to use his private property as "a mobile billboard" for the state's message was a violation of his First Amendment right to not promote an idea he found morally repugnant, and his conviction was overturned.

A conservative and an observant Jehovah's Witness, Maynard was represented by the American Civil Liberties Union, who, he said, "does a good job for good things . . . and a good job for bad things. . . . But they did right by me."

Suicide Help Line

CONSENT TO DEATH

14. No person is entitled to consent to have death inflicted on him (Canada Criminal Code, § 14).

8

Judges, Lawyers, and the Law

The strangeness of our laws won't surprise those familiar with the quirks of the people and procedures involved in their making. Here we read of the more curious aspects of lawyers, laws, and the legal establishment—from their occasional warping of time and space to their more frequent subversion of the English language to their fashion faux pas.

Time Bomb

They do tricks even I can't figure out.

—Harry Houdini, magician

The following is a tax law currently in effect in Australia:

DIVISION 165—ANTIAVOIDANCE

The Commissioner may:

(a) treat a particular event that actually happened as not having happened, and

(b) treat a particular event that did not actually happen as having happened and . . .

(c) treat a particular event that actually happened as:

(1) having happened at a time different from the time it actually happened (A New Tax System (Goods and Services Tax) Act 1999 (Australia)).

Mad Men

You can't be shining lights at the Bar because you are too kind . . . you are not cold blooded. You have not a high grade of intellect. I doubt you can ever make a living.

—Clarence Darrow, prominent American attorney, to women's lawyers group in Chicago, 1895

Shortly after the first woman in the United States was admitted to the bar, Rhoda Lavinia Goodell began arguing cases in front of the Wisconsin circuit court, normally the single prerequisite for being allowed to argue before the state's highest court. But the learned men of the Wisconsin Supreme Court denied Ms. Goodell's application, with Chief Justice Ryan authoring the opinion:

We cannot but think the common law wise in excluding women from the profession of the law. . . . The law of

nature destines and qualifies the female sex for the bear-
ing and nurture of children . . . callings of women, incon-
sistent with those radical and sacred duties . . . are
departures from the order of nature, and when volun-
tary, treason against it.

The peculiar qualities of womanhood, its gentle
graces . . . its purity, its delicacy, its emotional impulses,
its subordination of hard reason to sympathetic feel-
ing, are surely not qualifications for forensic strife. . . .
Womanhood is moulded for gentler and better things (In
the Matter of the Motion to Admit Ms. Lavinia Goodell
to the Bar of This Court, 39 Wis. 232 (1875)).

Ms. Goodell eventually turned to the legislature, which in
1877 passed a bill prohibiting gender-based denial of bar
admissions. Her second application to practice in front of
the Wisconsin Supreme Court was granted in 1879, over
the vehement dissent of Chief Justice Ryan.

Eurojargon

The European Union, consisting of twenty-seven member
states, is the biggest and busiest lawmaking body in the
history of the world. Established in 1993, the EU has created both a vast bureaucracy and a secret language to service it. A recent EU publication helpfully distinguishes
between Eurojargon and Eurospeak but itself finds that
they're equally incomprehensible.

The language gap between the EU and the world at large
has grown so large that many EU agencies now publish

glossaries of their own newly invented words. *Twinning*, for example, is defined as "the secondment of experts from member states to the administrations of the candidate countries," and an *action plan* "furthers progress in the priority areas that the Accession Partnerships have pinpointed." The EU's new math, *variable-geometry Europe*, describes "the idea of a method of differentiated integration which acknowledges that there are irreconcilable differences within the integration structure."

Now there are *majorities* and *absolute majorities* and also *qualified majorities*, *reinforced qualified majorities*, and *double majorities*. Committees may review *non-papers* and then practice *comitology*, *automaticity*, *communitization*, *deconcentration*, *subsidiarity*, and even old-fashioned *social dialogue*, all to achieve such laudable goals as *flexicurity* and *deepening*.

One EU phrase that does have real meaning is *democratic deficit*, defined in their glossary as having become increasingly "inaccessible to the ordinary citizen because their method of operating is so complex."

An Act to Prevent Maiming and Wounding

An Act to Prevent Maiming and Wounding, first drafted in England in 1670, was later adopted by many American states. The intent behind the law is still in force today, often with much of the original wording almost intact, and the horse trading behind this ancient legislation bears a striking resemblance to the smoke-filled legislative chambers of our own age.

In 1670, Sir John Coventry cracked wise about the king's romantic life and was assaulted by Sir Thomas Sandys and his men, who slit his nose. The incident caused a sensation and triggered a push for new legislation addressed to injuries that were serious but did not cripple a man or render him less able to fight his adversaries.

According to the bill's written history, on January 24, 1671, the House of Commons met, and a bill drawn by the House of Lords was read to chambers. A resolution was passed that debate of the bill should be adjourned to the next day. On January 25, the first amendment to the Second Reading of the Amendments was read a second time, and a second amendment was read a second time, and then debated, and it was resolved that the amendment be postponed and that a report be issued.

The next amendment, relating to the former amendment, was read a second time, and referred to committee. The fourth and fifth amendments were read twice, and the sixth amendment read a second time. That amendment passed in the negative. It was then resolved that the word *nose* be inserted, and the phrases *cut off a nose or lip* and *or joint* also be inserted, and all were passed in the negative.

The seventh amendment was read a second time, and passed in the negative, and the eighth as well. The House was then adjourned for the day. The next day, a report about the amendments was received from the committee to which the amendments had been committed. The committee saw no reason to agree with the Lords to the two amendments postponed, and the reasons were to be offered to a conference with the Lords, to justify the amendments of the House made to the Lords' amendments. The amendments were agreed to, but a conference was desired about the amendments, and the Lords agreed to the conference, which was to be attended by members who had formerly been appointed to prepare reasons.

The Reasons for Amendments were delivered at the conference with the Lords, while the Committee of Privileges was ordered to meet on the next Saturday. The House was then adjourned for the day. The bill, An Act to Prevent Maiming and Wounding (22, 23 Car. II.c.1), was eventually enacted:

> By this statute it is enacted that if any person, of malice aforethought, and by laying in wait, unlawfully cut or disable the tongue, put out an eye, slit the nose, cut off the nose or lip, or cut off or disable any limb, or member of the other person, with intent to maim or disfigure him, such person, his counselors, aider and abettors, shall be guilty of a felony, without benefit of clergy.

The Rule Against Perpetuities

The Rule against Perpetuities prohibits "a grant of an estate unless the interest must vest, if at all, no later than 21 years (plus a period of gestation to cover a posthumous birth) after the death of some person alive when interest was created" (*Black's Law Dictionary*).

The concise wording belies the rule's main claim to fame: its utter incomprehensibility. Among lawyers, the rule is considered the most complex law in all of law, so misunderstood that a lawyer who accidentally violates it is deemed not to have committed legal malpractice. In a 1961 California case often cited by frustrated law students, the court dismissed a legal malpractice claim against an attorney accused of having violated the rule, finding that even reasonably competent lawyers can't be expected to understand it (*Lucas v. Hamm*, 56 Cal. 2d 583, Cal. 196).

The rule was designed to curb a person's ability to distribute assets to remote ancestors years after he died, the "Dead Hand," and to eventually put chunks of wealth and property back in circulation. The rule remains in effect in most states and countries, although several bizarre outcomes are possible, including the problematic "fertile octogenarian" and "unborn widow" scenarios.

The difficulty of the rule is borne out in the screenplay of steamy movie classic *Body Heat*, where, at the request of Matty, his double-crossing lover, attorney Ned Racine murders her husband. Investigators question Ned about his lover's sudden windfall, arising from his mishandling of her dead husband's will:

RACINE: I'm confused, too. Do you have a problem with the witnessing or the signatures? What is it you're getting at?

HARDIN: No, there doesn't seem to be any problem there. This is Edmund Walker's last will and testament. I'm afraid the problem is elsewhere. . . . In writing the will, I'm afraid Mr. Racine violated what's known as "the rule against perpetuities." . . . It's a small thing, but it's the law. It forbids an inheritance to be passed down indefinitely for generations. Many general practitioner lawyers don't fully understand it.

Objection to Form

Defendant filed a document titled "Defendant's Motion to Discharge Response to Plaintiff's Response to Defendant's Response Opposing Objection to Discharge." The judge denied the motion, in a decision titled, "Order Denying Motion for Incomprehensibility" (*In re King*, Case No. 05-56485-C, Bankruptcy Court, Texas (2006)).

Indictment

Henderson was charged with stealing electronics from a MAACO garage, but that was too simple for the district attorney, who, according to the court, "never uses one word when two or three will do just as well." In the indictment, the word *burglariously* appeared three times.

At a hearing to determine whether the document should be thrown out as too confusing, expert witness Ann Dreher, an English teacher, testified that "consistent with accepted rules of English grammar, the indictment did not charge Jacob Henderson with anything." Actually, she testified, the indictment accused the electronics of breaking, entering, and stealing themselves.

On appeal, a nine-judge panel had to decide whether it was Henderson or the gadgets that were charged with the crime. Carefully reviewing the placement of a period, the court held that, according to the indictment "merchandise, not Jacob Henderson, burglarized the Maaco Paint Shop on

May 15, 1982." The state conceded the "patently inappropriate period" but said the document should stand anyway.

The court ultimately sustained the indictment, finding that it gave sufficient notice to the defendant of the crimes he was charged with, despite the bad grammar (*Henderson v. State, Supreme Court of Mississippi*, 445 So.2d 1364 (1984)).

Pseudo Absurdia

At a 1997 robing ceremony, newly appointed Superior Court Judge Patrick Couwenberg was introduced to an appreciative public. His background included the army *and* navy, service in Vietnam, a Purple Heart, the best schools, and prestigious law firms.

When a local newspaper questioned his qualifications, the well-connected judge and self-proclaimed war hero bullied a weak-kneed court system for three and a half years, all the while ruling over other people's lives and fates from his sixth-floor courtroom.

The judge defended himself at a series of hearings where he was represented by no less than three attorneys, but a forty-seven-page decision still found him to be a pathological liar unsuited for the bench. The phony Purple Heart and shrapnel to the groin? Couwenberg explained that he really was in the Naval Reserve and could theoretically have seen action, though he didn't. Degrees from prestigious Cal Poly and Loyola? No, but he had attended unaccredited Chaffey Junior College, and La Verne Law School. And he did pass the California bar exam, though it took him six tries.

As to the written applications, Couwenberg explained his wife typed up the forms, and he didn't bother to check, and, anyway, it was his view that education was irrelevant to a judicial application. When he fudged his bar exam failures, it was because he saw failing the bar five times as "something positive." Of his "undercover work" with the CIA, of course the witness from the CIA would deny it. And when asked why he said nothing while his fanciful biography was read publicly during his swearing-in ceremony, he said he thought the ceremony was more in the nature of "a humorous roast."

The judge also offered the testimony of three medical and psychological experts, one of whom testified that Couwenberg suffered from "pseudologia fantastica," a condition "manifested by 'story-telling that often has a sort of matrix of fantasy.'" How this qualified him to be a judge was left unexplained.

Pseudo-whatever or just plain sociopath, Couwenberg was finally removed from the bench in late 2001.

Ash Receivers, Tobacco (Desk Type)

In 1993, the General Services Agency, which distributes goods to government agencies, used nine pages to describe the precise dimensions, color, polish, and markings required for government-issue "ash receivers, tobacco (desk type)," more commonly known as ashtrays.

A minimum of four cigarette rests, spaced equidistant around the periphery and aimed at the center of the receiver, molded into the top. The cigarette rests shall be sloped toward the center of the ash receiver. The rests shall be parallel to the outside top edge of the receiver or in each corner, at the manufacturer's option. All surfaces shall be smooth.

TESTING

The test shall be made by placing the specimen on its base upon a solid support (a 1¾ inch, 44.5mm maple plank), placing a steel center punch (point ground to a 60-degree included angle) in contact with the center of the inside surface of the bottom and striking with a hammer in successive blows of increasing severity until breakage occurs. . . . The specimen should break into a small number of irregular shaped pieces not greater in number than 35, and it must not dice. . . . Any piece ¼ inch (6.4 mm) or more on any three of its adjacent edges (excluding the thickness dimension) shall be included in the number counted. Smaller fragments shall not be counted.

The regulation has since been repealed (Regulation AA-A-710E (superseding Regulation AA-A-710D)).

Send in the Clown

U.S. Supreme Court justices used to wear red robes and wigs but discarded the wigs and changed to plain black robes. In

1995, Chief Justice Rehnquist was impressed with the costumes he saw at a Gilbert and Sullivan comic opera and undertook to personally design and wear a robe with brilliant gold stripes, a style that the other justices refused to adopt.

But Rehnquist's taste in clothes was always suspect; introduced to President Nixon while wearing a pink shirt and psychedelic tie, Nixon said, "Is he Jewish? He looks it. That's a hell of a costume he's wearing, just like a clown."

Meso Madness

Victims of mesothelioma are the targets of a bizarre Internet subculture whose evolving twists and turns make *meso* among the most lucrative words in the world.

Mesothelioma is a deadly lung disease nearly always caused by exposure to asbestos, and the basis of tens of thousands of lawsuits. Because virtually no one has an interest in the disease except actual or claimed victims, Internet clicks on websites using the word *mesothelioma* reveal a ready customer base for lawyers eager to snare cases. The cases are especially prized because they can be cheaply processed in assembly-line fashion, often by paralegals and lower-paid staff, and because most settle with minimum fuss and maximum profit.

How much lawyers pay for a meso click referral varies. In 2007, a single click on *mesothelioma attorney Texas* went for $65.21, while *asbestos attorney* was a relative bargain at $51.68. *Malignant mesothelioma* went for $44.87, while *pleural mesothelioma* cost $43.50, and just plain *mesothelioma* $50.04.

At these prices, a vast array of brokers, middlemen, and hangers-on have created websites and sold the clicks to interested parties; nowadays competition is so fierce that a new wave of meso-mongers has metastasized-keyword advisers, misspelling specialists, link farms, splogs, zombies, and meso arbitragers, all trying to grab their piece of the meso pie.

Attorneys can seek meso victims directly through their own websites, often disguised as "information centers." Competition is now so tough that one of the nation's leading meso advertisers recently hired click fraud detectives to identify competitors who were clicking on their site just to drive their advertising costs up.

Baron & Budd P.C. of Texas, "Protecting What's Right," has one of the more popular meso sites but is better known for its off-line contributions to meso law.

In 1997, a worksheet used by the firm to "prepare" clients for depositions was accidentally disclosed. Much of the memo was addressed to product identification, a key issue in any meso case:

> "*Remember to say you saw the NAMES on the CANS*"

> "*. . . you NEVER saw any labels . . . that said WARNING or DANGER.*"

> "*Be CONFIDENT that you saw just as much of one brand as all the others. All the manufacturers in your case should share the blame equally.*"

A "rogue" paralegal took the fall, political donations were made, and the firm's attorneys emerged unscathed.

B & B retained William Hodes, top legal ethicist and author of *Two Cheers for Lying (About Immaterial Matters).*

As Mr. Hodes succinctly explained in his book, "It is . . . appropriate for a lawyer to instruct his client how to answer questions in accordance with the truth that will best serve his case."

Shit Happens

The following is from the Canadian Criminal Code:

> WILLFULLY CAUSING EVENT TO OCCUR
>
> *429. (1) Every one who causes the occurrence of an event by doing an act . . . knowing that the act . . . will probably cause the occurrence of the event . . . whether the event occurs or not, shall be deemed . . . to have caused the occurrence of the event (§ 429).*

Dream On

Sleeping through trial and possibly even the crime itself occurs in a small but significant number of cases.

Hardworking judges deserve their rest. Renowned Lord Thankerton was known for taking a nap and knitting during court sessions. In Australia, it took the High Court to overturn a criminal conviction despite a judge's loud snoring during trial; the jury snickered and courtroom employees dropped heavy documents to try to wake him up (*Cesan v. The Queen* (2008) HCA 52). Nevada judge Elizabeth Halverson fell asleep during her very first criminal trial and was later removed from the bench; in 2009, her husband went to jail for hitting her on the head with a frying pan.

Deathly bored lawyers defending cases in which their clients' lives are literally on the line can grab a few winks, and the conviction may or may not be overturned. A new trial was ordered for Calvin Burdine, minutes away from execution, because his lawyer snoozed during the trial—he's now serving life (*Burdine v. Johnson*, 262 F.3d 336 (Fifth Circ. 2001)). But George McFarland's conviction was upheld despite his lawyer having slept through jury selection and more deeply during trial (*McFarland v. State*, 928 S.W.2d 482 (Tex. Crim. App. 1996)).

Many defendants have slept during their alleged crimes, or so they've claimed. According to an expert witness hired by the *prosecution* in a recent British murder case where the defendant was acquitted, at least sixty-eight murders have been committed while sleepwalking.

In 1859, loving mother Esther Griggs tossed her baby girl Lizzie out the window—physical evidence and Griggs's confused ramblings supported her claim that she dreamed the house was on fire; baby Lizzie survived. In 1989, Canadian Ken Parks drove ten miles to his in-laws' home, killed his mother-in-law, and then turned himself in at the police station. He claimed he was sleepwalking, as he had done in the past, and was acquitted by a jury. An appeals court upheld the acquittal, describing his sleepwalking as "non-insane automatism."

A sleepwalking defense doesn't always work—in 1998, British chef Dean Sokell claimed his claw-hammer assault on wife, Eleni, was done while sleepwalking but admitted he stabbed her to death after he awoke—he's in jail for life.

And widely reported but not fully authenticated: In the 1800s, French detective Robert Ledru was asked to investigate a murder on the beach. When he examined footprints and the fatal bullet, he concluded that he himself had committed the crime, while sleepwalking, and turned himself in.

Bad Move

TIME WHEN THEFT COMPLETED

(2) A person commits theft when . . . he moves it or causes it to move or to be moved, or begins to cause it to become movable (Canada Civil Code, § 322).

Ordinary People

Even if he [Supreme Court nominee G. Harold Carswell] is mediocre, there are a lot of mediocre judges and people and lawyers. They are entitled to a little representation, aren't they . . . ?

—Senator Roman Hruska, speech to the U.S. Senate, 1970

According to articles in the prestigious *University of Chicago Law Review*, either Gabriel Duvall or Thomas Todd are the most trivial and insignificant Supreme Court justices of all time.

Professor David P. Currie nominated Gabriel Duvall, who "achieved an enviable standard of insignificance against which all other Justices must be measured." In twenty-three years on the High Court, Justice Duvall wrote only seventeen opinions and dissented from powerful Chief Justice John Marshall only twice.

Frank H. Easterbrook, chief judge of the U.S. Court of Appeals, Seventh Circuit, appointed Thomas Todd, a former land surveyor who in nineteen years on the bench wrote only fourteen opinions, almost all concerning land survey claims.

Little more can be said about either (*University of Chicago Law Review* 50, no. 2 (1983): 466–496).

Raising a Stink

The *Clameur de Haro*, an ancient legal procedure still employed in the Channel Islands off England, allows the court to stop an alleged wrongdoer from continuing the disputed activity.

During a Clameur, the "Criant," before at least two witnesses and the defendant, bends down on his knees, recites the Lord's Prayer in French, and says, *"Haro! Haro! Haro! A mon aide mon Prince, on me fait tort"* (Hear me! Hear me! Hear me! Come to my aid, my Prince, for someone does me wrong).

Channel Islanders have clung steadfast to their legal traditions even in the face of fearsome struggle. In 1990, the island of Sark was invaded by a heavily armed, unemployed French nuclear physicist who the day before posted flyers announcing his intention to storm the island, and was then arrested while sitting on a bench by the island's volunteer constable; this heroic defense preserved for all the venerable tradition of *Clameur de Haro*.

Headhunting

British women in the hands of a trusted hairdresser may get a divorce attorney along with their usual cut and color.

In 2006, the top-rated Trethowan law firm, founded in 1866, began sending letters to hair salons with the headline, "We'll pay you 75 pounds per referred case!" The letter told salon owners that six out of ten marriages ended in divorce, and, according to *London's Daily Mail Online* newspaper, continued:

> *In the hairdressing profession . . . some clients may feel comfortable discussing personal issues while receiving treatment. In many instances you may provide a listening ear. At other times you might feel able to recommend them on to someone who can help them out.*

Criticized for inappropriate solicitation of clients, the law firm withdrew the letter.

Let It Be

A Canadian criminal statute:

> *Order Recommending That Each Entity Listed as of July 23, 2006 in the Regulations Establishing a List of*

*Entities Remain a Listed Entity (Canada Criminal Code,
Enabling Statute, SI/2006-133).*

Quis Custodiet Ipso Custodes
(Who's Watching the Watchers?)

Presiding over juvenile court in 2002, Pennsylvania judges
Conahan and Ciavarella decided to trade kids for cash.
With Conahan handling the paperwork and Ciavarella the
sentencing, the enterprising duo shut down the county jail
and remanded kids charged with minor infractions to
private jails in which the two held a secret ownership interest, earning an estimated $2 million.

The scheme hinged on handing down the longest, most
profitable sentences possible, and law-and-order man Ciavarella lived up to his no-nonsense reputation, jailing kids
like honor student Hillary Transue, who published a spoof
of the assistant principal on her MySpace page and was
promptly handcuffed and jailed for three months.

Both judges pleaded guilty and are serving lengthy
prison sentences, not in jails they own.

Stranglehold

In 1971, Texas legislator Tom Moore Jr., fed up with his
colleagues' willingness to pass virtually any bill that was
proposed, sponsored a resolution honoring the Boston
Strangler, citing devotion to his work and his contribu-

tions as an acknowledged leader in his singular field. The resolution was passed unanimously by the House of Representatives, then immediately withdrawn by Moore.

All Atwitter

Texting and tweeting is setting courtrooms atwitter as jurors and even witnesses let their fingers do the talking.

Sky Development CEO Gavin Sussman texted a company executive for advice while he was on the witness stand; the judge promptly declared a mistrial. Susan Henwood texted her homebound husband about the progress of a collection case against him. "They're coming for the Polaris Ranger," she said, earning herself a thirty-day jail sentence.

Stoam Holdings moved to retry an unfavorable 2009 verdict after a juror posted eight tweets during and after trial, one of them reading, "I just gave away TWELVE MILLION DOLLARS of somebody else's money." The juror claimed he did nothing wrong but a recent tweet said, "Well, I'm off to see the judge. Hope they don't lock me under the jail."

Equally misguided jurors are now doing their own online searches for justice, Googling everything from drive times to witness biographies to medical conditions, none subject to tests of accuracy or cross-examination. State officials are now drafting instructions explaining to jurors why they should ignore the latest technology and concentrate on old-fashioned testimony given by actual people in a real courtroom.

Running with Scissors

Squabbling lawyers couldn't agree on where to hold a deposition. A frustrated judge directed the parties to convene at a neutral site and, if they couldn't agree, to meet on the federal courthouse steps. He then directed:

> Each lawyer shall be entitled to be accompanied by one paralegal who shall act as an attendant and witness. At that time and location, counsel shall engage in one (1) game of rock, paper, scissors." The winner of this engagement shall be entitled to select the location (Avista Management Inc. v. Wausau Underwriters Insurance, No. 6105-cv 1430, Orlando, Florida (2006)).

Double Indemnity

In the classic case of *Garratt v. Dailey*, 46 Wash 2d 197 (Wash 1955), Ms. Garratt claimed she was injured when five-year-old Brian Dailey deliberately pulled a chair out from under her as she was about to sit in it, while the boy said that in moving the chair he had no malicious intent. The trial court found the boy had no intent to cause harm and dismissed the case, but an appeals court ruled that an assault could be based on the boy's knowledge of likely harm, even without an intent to harm.

Years later, a law professor and author of the legal journal articles "Putting Students Where They Belong" and "Déjà Vu All Over Again" reenacted the seminal case. In front of a first-year torts class, a law student who was said to have skipped the day's assignment and thus ignorant of the *Garratt* case was asked by the professor to step to the front of the lecture hall and invited to sit in a chair, which he promptly pulled out from under her. The student's skirt flew up, she hit the ground hard, and she reinjured a recently operated-on back. A 2005 settlement of the lawsuit scuttled the intriguing scenario of the professor's liability being judged on concepts derived from the very case he was teaching at the time of the incident (*"Jane Doe" v. Pace University Law School et al., New York*).

Whigging Out

For heavens sake discard the monstrous wig which makes English judges look like rats.

—Thomas Jefferson, American president

In 2008, the English judiciary decided to abandon centuries of sartorial tradition in favor of more modern attire for judges and lawyers.

Surveys found British lawyers and judges deemed out of touch by the people they served, and the sartorial change was primarily sponsored by powerful Lord Phillips, who favored Velcro fasteners. Bareheaded solicitors who appeared in court beside gloriously bewigged barristers also supported the change, wanting wigs for themselves or no wigs at all.

Judges were peeved at what some called Trekkie-style robes with hard-to-reach pockets, but an authoritative fashion editor said the robe "ticks all the right fashion boxes but remains cerebral enough to invoke respect in the courtroom."

Criminal judges will continue to wear horsehair wigs, costing between $1,200 and $3,000, but not civil and family court judges, who were said to have scared little children.

Lately, U.S. Supreme Court justices have taken to wearing black skullcaps on formal occasions.

Signed, Sealed, and Delivered

Belford University is one of the world's largest mail-order universities and offers the same juris doctor degree as any traditional law school. According to its website, seventy-two thousand fully accredited university students have matriculated to date, and Belford is accredited by both the IAAOU and the UCOEA. Its educational credo is that students be allowed to proceed at their own pace, on their own schedule, at their own convenience.

An applicant for admission, after consultation with university advisers and the filing of detailed application forms, is carefully reviewed by an evaluation committee. Applicants also file an additional form specifying their final GPA, and candidates feeling they lack more formal or traditional academic qualifications may take an online equivalency test based on prior knowledge or, if none, life experience.

A response from the committee is received immediately, and if acceptance is granted, tuition arrangements are made. For the convenience of matriculating students,

Belford offers a flexible payment plan, no credit card is required, and they offer free express delivery via DHL. A juris doctor candidate who meets all requirements is granted a law degree within just fifteen days, guaranteed, and the diploma will be printed with a gold-plated seal, along with two transcripts, one award of excellence and one certificate of distinction.

In 2007, New York City Fire Department employees with degrees from Belford University were arrested for the fraudulent filing of their job applications. A suspicious Fire Department investigator filed his own Belford application, declaring his qualification for an engineering degree to be, "I luv planes and rockets." The investigator was awarded a degree in aerospace engineering with highest honors.

Selected Bibliography

The following is a small selection of the many hundreds of sources; precise citations of more modern statutes are cited in the text. A few more listings concern items of historical interest or with more obscure sources.

Don't Dent That Ox

Steele, Frances R. "The Code of Lipit-Ishtar." University of Pennsylvania Museum. *American Journal of Archeology* 2, no. 2 (July–September 1948): 3–28.

The Murder Act

Block, Brian, and John Hostettler. *Hanging in the Balance*. Winchester, England: Waterside Press, 1997.

"1803: George Foster, and Thence to the Re-animator" (post by dogboy). January 18, 2009. Executed Today Blog, www.execut edtoday.com/2009/01/18/1803-george-foster-giovanni-aldini -galvanic-reanimation (accessed May 3, 2009).

Johnson, Arthur Charles, ed. *The Complete Newgate Calendar*. Vol. 4 of *Law in Popular Culture Collection* by G. T. Crook. University of Texas Law School Austin, Tarlton Law Library: Jamail Center for Legal Research, 1926.

Johnson, D. R. "Introductory Anatomy: Introduction" (course notes). University of Leeds, Department of Biological Sciences, n.d. www.leeds.ac.uk/chb/lectures/anatomy1.html (accessed May 6, 2009).

"The Old Bailey." *Old and New London: Vol. 2* (1878): 461–477. www.british-history.ac.uk/report.aspx?compid=45115 (accessed May 6, 2009).

Pilkington, Mark. "Sparks of Life." *Guardian*, October 7, 2004. www.guardian.co.uk/education/2004/oct/07/research.highereducation1 (accessed May 3, 2009).

Pleas of the Manor of Abbey

Halsall, Paul. "Manors of the Abbey of Bec, AD 1246." From F. W. Maitland, ed. *Select Pleas in Manorial and Other Seigniorial Courts: Volume 1—Reigns of Henry VIII and Edward I* (London: Bernard Quaritch, 1889). www.fordham.edu/halsall/seth/bec.html (accessed October 11, 2009).

Babylmania

"The Code of Hammurabi." *Gavel2Gavel*. www.re-quest.net/g2g/historical/laws/hammurabi (accessed December 17, 2008).

Johns, Claude Herman Walters. "Babylonian Law: The Code of Hammurabi." *Encyclopedia Britannica*, 11th ed. Yale Law School Lillian Goldman Law Library: The Avalon Project, 1910–1911. http://avalon.law.yale.edu/ancient/hammpre.asp (accessed July 7, 2009).

That Girl

Halsall, Paul. "The Questioning of John Rykener: A Male Cross Dressing Prostitute, 1395." May 1998. Internet Medieval Sourcebook, www.fordham.edu/halsall/source/1395rykener.html (accessed April 2, 2009).

Tennis, Anyone?

Curtis, Kennith R., Merry E. Wiesner, and William Bruce Wheeler. *Discovering the Medieval Past: A Look at the Evidence*. Boston: Houghton Mifflin, 2003.

Frankly Absurd

Drew, Katherine Fischer. *The Laws of the Salian Franks (Pactus legis Salicae).* Philadelphia: University of Pennsylvania Press, 1991.

Halsall, Paul. "The Law of Salian Franks." February 1996. Internet Medieval Sourcebook, www.fordham.edu/halsall/source/salic -law.html (accessed March 31, 2009).

Henderson, Ernest F. "The Salic Law." In *Select Historical Documents of the Middle Ages.* London: George Bell, 1910.

Pyramid Scheme

Andrews, Mark. "Law and the Legal System in Ancient Egypt." Tour Egypt, www.touregypt.net/featurestories/law.htm (accessed March 22, 2009).

Dollinger, Andre. "An Introduction to the History and Culture of Egypt." www.reshafim.org.il/ad/egypt/index.html (accessed February 22, 2009).

Friedman, David. "Predominant Concepts of Justice and Jurisprudence in Ancient Egyptian Law" (academic paper). www.davidd friedman.com/Academic/Course_Pages/legal_systems_very_ different/egyptian_law_paper.htm (accessed July 16, 2009).

Parsons, Marie. "Deir el-Medina." Tour Egypt, www.touregypt.net/ featurestories/medina.htm (accessed March 22, 2009).

The Judgment of the Pillory

Halsall, Paul. "The Assizes of Bread, Beer & *Lucrum Pistoris.*" August 1998. Internet Medieval Sourcebook, www.fordham.edu/halsall/ source/breadbeer.html (accessed September 8, 2009).

———. "The Judgment of the Pillory." August 1998. Internet Medieval Sourcebook, www.fordham.edu/halsall/source/judgepillory .html (accessed July 27, 2009).

A Forest of His Own

Reilly, S. A. *Our Legal Heritage.* Teddington, England: Echo Library, 2007.

The Laws Divine

Friedman, Lawrence M. *A History of American Law*, 3rd ed. New York: Touchstone, 1973 (revised 2001).

Konig, Thomas. "Dale's Laws and Non-Common Law Origins of Criminal Justice in Virginia." *American Journal of Legal History* 26, no. 4 (1982): 354.

Pleas at Northampton

Halsall, Paul. "Pleas at Northampton in the Fourth Year of the Reign of King John." From F. W. Maitland, ed. *Select Pleas of the Crown: Volume 1—AD 1200–1225* (London: Bernard Quaritch, 1888). www.fordham.edu/halsall/seth/pleas-northamptoneyre.html (accessed July 27, 2009).

Red Menace

Dewey, H. W., trans. "The Sudebnik." 1996. Bucknell University Russian Studies Department. www.departments.bucknell.edu/russian/const/sudebnik.html (accessed July 18, 2009).

Duhaime, Lloyd. "1016: The Russkaia Pravda." March 4, 2008. Duhaime.org, http://duhaime.org/LawMuseum/LawArticle-294/1016-The-Russkaia-Pravda.aspx (accessed June 21, 2009).

Padokh, Yaroslav. "Ruskaia Pravda." *Encyclopedia of Ukraine*, vol. 4 (1993). www.encyclopediaofukraine.com/pages/R/U/Ruskaia PravdaIT.htm (accessed July 18, 2009).

"Ruskaia Pravda." *Russian Primary Chronicle*. www.dur.ac.uk/a.k .harrington/russprav.html (accessed June 21, 2009).

Time After Time

"Text 213: 1449: C49/27/14: Petition of Commons That Priests Be Pardoned for All Accusations of Rape." *An Anthology of Chancery English*. University of Virginia Library. http://etext.lib.virginia .edu/toc/modeng/public/AnoChan.html (accessed October 11, 2009).

No Guns for Jews

Hatch, Orrin G. "The Right to Keep and Bear Arms: Report of the Subcommittee on the Constitution of the Committee on the Judiciary." Testimony for the U.S. Senate Judiciary Committee. U.S. Senate Ninety-Seventh Congress, Second Session, February 1982.

Orlando, Linda. "Ireland Abolishes Thousands of Bizarre Colonial Laws." April 3, 2006. Buzzle.com. www.buzzle.com/editorials/4 -3-2006-92549.asp (accessed October 21, 2009).

Stephenson, Carl, and Frederick George Marcham, eds. *Sources of English Constitutional Law: A Selection of Documents from AD 600 to the Present.* Cornell University. New York: Harper & Row, 1937. www.constitution.org/sech/sech_.htm (accessed October 11, 2009).

Putting on the Ritz

Blackwood's Edinburgh Magazine 48 (July–December 1840). Edinburgh: William Blackwood and Sons, 1840, p. 264. http://books .google.com/books?id=LG4o6Wa8pFQC&printsec=titlepage& output=html (accessed May 10, 2009).

Lee, Sidney, ed. *Dictionary of National Biography* 31. England: Kent & Co. Publisher, 1859, pp. 65–66. www.archive.org/stream/ dictionarynatio47stepgoog#page/n78/mode/2up (accessed August 29, 2009).

Reeves, John, and W. F. Finalson. *Reeves' History of the English Law.* Philadelphia: Murphy, 1880.

Upside-Down Tricks and Crisscross Maneuvers

McKnight, Brian, and T. C. Liu James, trans. *The Enlightened Judgments: Ch'ing-Ming Chi—The Sung Dynasty Collection.* SUNY Series in Chinese Philosophy and Culture. New York: State University of New York Press, 1999.

The Extermination of the Clan McGregor

Bettinger, Blaine. "Using DNA to Reunite the Clan Gregor." June 13, 2007. Genetic Genealogist Blog, www.thegeneticgenealogist.com/ 2007/06/13/using-dna-to-reunite-the-clan-gregor (accessed June 5, 2009).

MacGregor, Amelia Georgina Murray. *History of the Clan Gregor from Public Records and Private Collections; Comp. at the Request of the Clan Gregor Society: Volume First.* Edinburgh: William Brown, 1898. Internet Archive of American Libraries, www .archive.org/stream/historyclangreg00socigoog#page/n8/ mode/2up (accessed June 5, 2009).

MacLeay, Kenneth. *Historical Memoirs of Rob Roy and the Clan MacGregor: Including Original Notices of Lady Grange.* Edinburgh: William Brown, 1881.

McNaughton, Peter. "St. Fillians and the Stewarts of Ardvorlich." *Highland Strathearn Papers in a Trunk.* www.highlandstrathearn. com/content/stewarts-ardvorlich (accessed June 6, 2009).

Scott, Sir Walter. "Introduction and Postscript." In *A Legend of Montrose.* Literature Network, www.online-literature.com/walter_scott/ legend-of-montrose/0 (accessed June 6, 2009).

The Bawdy Courts

"Manuscripts and Special Collections: The Bawdy Court." Exhibition at the Weston Gallery, University of Nottingham. Cataloged by Jane Lunnon, February 24, 2009. www.nottingham.ac.uk/manu scriptsandspecialcollections/exhibitions/online/thebawdycourt/ introduction.aspx (accessed July 19, 2009).

Turley, Jonathan. "Of Lust and the Law." *Washington Post,* September 5, 2004. www.washingtonpost.com/wp-dyn/articles/A62581 -2004Sep4.html (accessed July 19, 2009).

Charlemagne the Pious

Halsall, Paul. "Charlemagne: Capitulary for Saxony, 775–790." January 1996. Internet Medieval Sourcebook, www.fordham.edu/ halsall/source/carol-Saxony.html (accessed July 27, 2009).

A Day in the Life . . .

"House of Lords Journal, Vol. 2: 27, October 1608." *Journal of the House of Lords* 2, 1578–1614 (1802): 542–543. British History Online, www.british-history.ac.uk/report.aspx?compid=28525 (accessed April 30, 2009).

Lex Loco

Nieuwenhuijsen, Kees C. "Lex Frisionum: Fine Amounts." August 2001. www.keesn.nl/lex/index.html (accessed June 7, 2009).

The Malefactor's Bloody Register

The Complete Newgate Calendar, Vol. 4 of *Law in Popular Culture Collection.* University of Texas Law School Austin, Tarlton Law

Library: Jamail Center for Legal Research. http://tarlton.law
.utexas.edu/lpop/etext/completenewgate.htm (accessed April 27,
2009).

Pleas—The Hundred of Triggshire

Halsall, Paul. "Select Pleas of the Crown: Pleas Before the Justices in
Eyre in the Reign of King John." From F. W. Maitland, ed. *Select
Pleas of the Crown: Volume 1—AD 1200–1225* (London: Bernard
Quaritch, 1888). www.fordham.edu/halsall/seth/pleas-cornish
.html (accessed July 27, 2009).

Through the Looking Glass

Browning, John G. "Legally Speaking: Irish Law—Ahead of Its Time."
Southeast Texas Record, July 11, 2007. www.setexasrecord.com/
arguments/197767-legally-speaking-irish-law----ahead-of-its
-time (accessed June 8, 2009).

Commissioners for Publishing the Ancient Laws and Institutes of
Ireland. *Ancient Laws and Institutes of Ireland.* Dublin: H. M.
Stationery Office, 1865. www.archive.org/details/ancientlaws01
hancuoft (accessed June 11, 2009).

Finney, Dee. *The Brehan Law.* April 17, 2001. www.greatdreams.com/
brehanlaw.htm (accessed June 6, 2009).

Ragan, Michael. *The Brehan Law.* 1999. www.danann.org/library/
law/breh2.html (accessed June 8, 2009).

Act Infinitum

Duhaime, Lloyd. *An Act Concerning Outlandish People Calling Themselves Egyptians*, "Crazy Laws—English Style (1482–1541)." August 9, 2008. Duhaime.org, http://duhaime.org/LawMuseum/
LawArticle-359/Crazy-Laws--English-Style-1482-1541.aspx (accessed June 12, 2009).

What an Ordeal!

Bartlett, Robert. "The Medieval Judicial Ordeal." In *Trial by Fire and
Water.* New York: Clarendon, 1986.

Halsall, Paul. "The Laws of King Athelstan, AD 924–939." June 1998.
Internet Medieval Sourcebook, www.fordham.edu/halsall/

source/560-975dooms.html#The%20Laws%20of%20King%20
Athelstan (accessed August 4, 2009).

———. "Ordeal Formulas." February 1996. Internet Medieval Sourcebook, www.fordham.edu/halsall/source/ordeals1.html (accessed
July 27, 2009).

———. "Ordeal of Boiling Water." January 1996. Internet Medieval
Sourcebook, www.fordham.edu/halsall/source/water-ordeal
.html (accessed July 27, 2009).

Close Shave

Caplan, Bryan. "Czarist Origins of Communism." George Mason
University. http://econfaculty.gmu.edu/bcaplan/museum/zarframe
.htm (accessed April 28, 2009).

Johnson, Matthew Raphael. "The Third Rome: Holy Russia, Tsarism
and Orthodoxy." Irvington-on-Hudson, NY: Foundation for Economic Liberty, 2004. Holy Trinity Orthodox School, www.holy
trinitymission.org/books/english/third_rome_m_johnson.htm
(accessed April 28, 2009).

Stanley, Diane. *Peter the Great.* New York: Morrow Junior Books,
1986.

Render unto Caesar

Adams, John Paul. "The Twelve Tables of Roman Law." www.csun
.edu/~hcfll004/12tables.html (accessed February 14, 2009).

Colson, Chuck. "Reasonably Necessary: Charitable Giving and Bankruptcy." *Christian Post*, December 29, 2006. www.christianpost
.com/opinion/columns/2006 (accessed February 16, 2009).

Halsall, Paul. "Ancient History Sourcebook: The Twelve Tables, c. 450
BCE." June 1998. Internet Ancient History Sourcebook, www
.fordham.edu/halsall/ancient/12tables.html (accessed February
16, 2009).

The Book of Dooms

Halsall, Paul. "The Anglo Saxon Dooms, 560–975." June 1998. Internet Medieval Sourcebook, www.fordham.edu/halsall/source/560
-975dooms.html (accessed June 6, 2009).

Thatcher, Oliver J., ed. *The Early Medieval World.* Vol. 4 of *The Library of Original Sources.* Milwaukee: University Research Extension, 1901.

Pleas at Lichfield

Halsall, Paul. "Staffordshire Eyre, AD 1203: Pleas at Lichfield in the Fifth Year of the Reign of King John." From F. W. Maitland, ed. *Select Pleas of the Crown: Volume 1—AD 1200–1225* (London: Bernard Quaritch, 1888). www.fordham.edu/halsall/seth/pleas -staffordeyre.html (accessed July 27, 2009).

Commune of Biella

Sella, Pietro. "The Statutes of the Commune of Bugelle (Biella) and the Documents Which Have Been Added." Italy: Biella at the Press of G. Testa, 1904. www.vialardi.org/VdSF/pdf/commune_ bugelle.pdf (accessed July 27, 2009).

Up to Code

Halsall, Paul. "The Code of Assura, c. 1075 BCE." July 1998. Internet Ancient History Sourcebook, www.fordham.edu/halsall/ancient/ 1075assyriancode.html (accessed March 31, 2009).

The Hittites of Hatti

Halsall, Paul. "The Code of the Nesilim, c. 1650–1500 BCE." August 1998. Internet Ancient History Sourcebook, www.fordham.edu/ halsall/ancient/1650nesilim.html (accessed March 31, 2009).

The Pleas of the Crown

"House of Commons Journal, Volume 9: 24 January 1671." *Journal of the House of Commons* 9, 1667–1687 (1802): 193. British History Online, www.british-history.ac.uk/source.aspx?pubid= 114&page=6&sort=1 (accessed May 1, 2009).

"House of Lords Journal, Volume 2: Note of Bills." *Journal of the House of Lords* 2, 1578–1614 (1802). British History Online, www.british -history.ac.uk/source.aspx?pubid=117&month=5&year=1614 (accessed May 1, 2009).

Maitland, F. W., ed. *Select Pleas of the Crown: Volume 1—AD 1200–1225.* London: Bernard Quaritch, 1888. Internet Archive of Canadian Li-

braries. www.archive.org/stream/publicationsofse01selduoft#page/
n11/mode/2up (accessed May 3, 2009).

The Scarlet Letter

Bouton, N., et al., eds. *New Hampshire Provincial, Town, and State
Papers: Vol. I, 1623–1686.* Concord & Nashua, NH: 1867, pp. 386–
409. Online Library of Liberty, A Project of Liberty Fund. http://
oll.libertyfund.org/?option=com_staticxt&staticfile
=show.php%3Ftitle=694&chapter=102333&layout=html
&Itemid=27 (accessed July 25, 2009).

Kane, J. *Famous First Facts: A Record of First Happenings, Discoveries,
and Inventions in American History*, 5th ed. New York: H. W.
Wilson, 1997, p. 77.

Lutz, Donald S., ed. *Colonial Origins of the American Constitution: A
Documentary History.* Indianapolis: Liberty Fund, 1998. Online
Library of Liberty, A Project of Liberty Fund. http://oll.liberty
fund.org/?option=com_staticxt&staticfile=show.php%3Ftitle=
694&Itemid=27 (accessed July 25, 2009).

Ward, Nathaniel. "Book of the General Lawes and Libertyes (1641)."
June 6, 2009. Duhaime.org, http://duhaime.org/LawMuseum/
LawArticle-594/Book-of-the-General-Lawes-and-Libertyes
-1641.aspx (July 27, 2009).

Pleas at Wapentake of Aswardhurn

Halsall, Paul. "Lincolnshire Eyre, AD 1202: Pleas at Lincoln in the
Fourth Year of the Reign of King John." From F. W. Maitland, ed.
Select Pleas of the Crown: Volume 1—AD 1200–1225 (London:
Bernard Quartich, 1888). www.fordham.edu/halsall/seth/pleas
-lincolneyre.html (accessed July 27, 2009).

When in Rome . . .

Scott, S. P., trans. *The Civil Law Including the Twelve Tables, the Insti-
tutes of Gaius, the Rules of Ulpian, the Opinions of Paulus, the
Enactments of Justinian, and the Constitutions of Leo.* Central
Trust Company, Estate of Samuel P. Scott, 1932.

A Remembrance of the Plague

Bell, Walter George. *The Great Plague in London in 1665*. London: John Lane, Bodley Head Press, 1924.

"Preface." *Analytical Index to the Series of Records Known as the Remembrancia, 1579–1664* (1878): iii–ix. British History Online, www.british-history.ac.uk/report.aspx?compid=59890 (accessed August 15, 2009).

Those Jews

Goddard, Hugh. *A History of Christian-Muslim Relations*. Chicago: New Amsterdam Books, 2000, p. 224.

Halsall, Paul. "Jews and the Later Roman Law 315–531 CE." July 1998. Jewish History Sourcebook, www.fordham.edu/halsall/jewish/jews-romanlaw.html (accessed April 6, 2009).

———. "Las Siete Partidas: Laws on Jews, 1254." October 1997. Internet Medieval Sourcebook, www.fordham.edu/halsall/source/jews-sietepart.html (accessed April 5, 2009).

———. "Pact of Umar, 7th Century." January 1996. Internet Medieval Sourcebook, www.fordham.edu/halsall/source/pact-umar.html (accessed April 5, 2009).

Scott, Samuel P., trans. *Las Siete Partidas of Alfanso X el Sabio*. New York: Commerce Clearing House, 1931.

Tritton, A. S. *The Caliphs and Their Non-Muslim Subjects: A Critical Study of the Covenant of Umar*. London: Frank Cass, 1970.

The Law Code of Gortyn

Halsall, Paul. "The Law Code of Gortyn (Crete)." August 1998. Internet Ancient History Sourcebook, www.fordham.edu/halsall/ancient/450-gortyn.html (accessed September 10, 2009).

Genghis

Albrecht, James F. "The Influence of the Great Code 'Yasa' on the Mongolian Empire." Professor, St. John's University. http://mypolice.ca/research_and_publications/MongolianLawCodeYasa.htm (accessed August 18, 2009).

Duhaime, Lloyd. "1206: The Yasak of Genghis Khan." January 3, 2009. Duhaime.org, http://duhaime.org/LawMuseum/LawArticle-519/

1206-The-Yasak-of-Genghis-Khan.aspx (accessed August 18, 2009).

Oestmoen, Per Inge. "The Yasa of Chingis Khan: A Code of Honor, Dignity and Excellence." www.coldsiberia.org/webdoc9.htm (accessed August 19, 2009).

Palmer, Joe. "Islamic Law and Genghis Khan's code." *Nth Position Online Magazine*, May 2003. www.nthposition.com/islamiclaw .php (accessed August 10, 2009).

Precise People

Gee, Henry, and William John Hardy, eds. *The King's Majesty's Declaration to His Loyal Subjects Concerning Lawful Sports to Be Used (1633).* Documents Illustrative of English Church History, Hanover Historical Texts Project. New York: Macmillan, 1896, pp. 428–432. http://history.hanover.edu/texts/engref/er93.html (accessed September 3, 2009).

Govett, L. A. *The King's Book of Sports: A History of the Declarations of King James I. and King Charles I. as to the Use of Lawful Sports on Sundays.* London, 1890.

James I/Charles I. *The King's Majesty's Declaration to His Subjects Concerning Lawful Sports to Be Used.* October 18, 1633. Norton Anthology of English Literature, www.wwnorton.com/college/ english/nael/17century/topic_3/sports.htm (accessed September 3, 2009).

Tait, James. "The Declaration of Sports for Lancashire." *English Historical Review* 32 (1917): 561–568. JSTOR, www.jstor.org/ pss/550860 (accessed September 10, 2009).

The Bloody Code

"James Belbin Burglary, 9th January 1788." *The Proceedings of the Old Bailey.* Ref: t17880109-11. Humanities Research Institute, University of Sheffield. www.oldbaileyonline.org/browse.jsp?id= t17880109-11&div=t17880109-11&terms=belbin#highlight (accessed March 22, 2009).

"Punishments at the Old Bailey: Late 17th Century to the Early 20th Century." *The Proceedings of the Old Bailey.* Humanities Research

Institute, University of Sheffield. www.oldbaileyonline.org/static/
Punishment.jsp (accessed March 22, 2009).

Volokh, Eugene. "Burglariously." August 1, 2007. Volokh Conspiracy,
http://volokh.com (accessed February 25, 2009).

The Spanking Machine

Bentham, Jeremy. *The Rationale of Punishment,* ed. James T. McHugh.
New York: Prometheus Books, 2008. (Originally pub. London:
Robert Heyward, 1830.)

Farrell, C. "The Spanking Machine: A Resilient Myth in Popular
Culture." Corpun: World Corporal Punishment Research, 2000.
www.corpun.com/machine.htm (accessed April 5, 2009).

Cattle Call

"George Soule in 17th Century Records." Plymouth, MA: Pilgrim
Hall Museum, 2005. www.pilgrimhall.org/soulegeorgerecords
.htm (accessed August 12, 2009).

"Plymouth Colony Division of Cattle, 1627." Plymouth Colony Archive
Project, 2000–2007. www.histarch.uiuc.edu/plymouth/cattlediv
.html (accessed August 8, 2009).

So Yesterday

Bahrampour, Tara. "A Brief Matter of Style." *Washington Post,*
February 11, 2005. www.washingtonpost.com/wp-dyn/articles/
A15387-2005Feb10.html (accessed April 1, 2009).

Gilleland, Michael. "Trousers." Herodotus 1.71.2-4 (quotation) and
Cicero, *Letters to His Friends* 9.15 (quotation). October 17, 2004.
Laudator Temporis Acti Blog, http://laudatortemporisacti.blog
spot.com/2004_10_01_archive.html (accessed March 27, 2009).

Jugge, R., and J. Cawood. "Concerning Ruffs, Hose, and Swords."
London: 1562. Elizabethan Sumptuary Statutes, July 14, 2001
(post by Maggi Ros). www.elizabethan.org/sumptuary/ruffs
-hose-swords.html (accessed March 12, 2009).

Lemieux, Pierre. "Lifestyles of the Tacky and Vulgar." *Western Standard,* March 14, 2005. www.pierrelemieux.org/artwsvirginia
.html (accessed April 1, 2009).

Swill Milk

Brown, Lucius P. "The Experience of New York City in Grading Market Milk." Read before General Session of the American Health Association, Rochester, New York, September 7, 1915. *American Journal of Public Health* 6, no. 7 (1916): 671–677. American Publix Health Association, www.ncbi.nlm.nih.gov/pmc/articles/PMC1286888 (accessed June 2, 2009).

Habstritt, Mary. "Manhattanville and New York City's Milk Supply." *Archive of Industry*, 2008. www.archiveofindustry.com/images/DairyNarrative.pdf (accessed May 25, 2009).

Wilson, Bee. "The Swill Is Gone." *New York Times*, September 29, 2008. Archives: "The Swill Milk Trade" (January 14, 1869); "Swill Milk Destroyed" (May 1, 1887).

The Master of the Revels

Kazuaki, Ota. "The Master of Revels and the Licensing of Late English Renaissance Drama [in Japanese]." *Journal of Studies in Languages and Cultures*, 51–64. National Institute of Informatics, Scholarly and Academic Information Navigator. http://ci.nii.ac.jp/naid/110000522848/en (accessed September 2, 2009).

Overall, W. H., and H. C. Overall, eds. "Plays and Players." *Analytical Index to the Series of Records Known as the Remembrancia: 1579–1664* (1878): 350–357. British History Online, www.british-history.ac.uk/source.aspx?pubid=581 (accessed September 2, 2009).

The Rule of Thumb

Adams, Cecil. "Does 'Rule of Thumb' Refer to an Old Law Permitting Wife Beating?" *Straight Dope*, May 12, 2000. www.straightdope.com/columns/read/2550/does-rule-of-thumb-refer-to-an-old-law-permitting-wife-beating (accessed March 3, 2009).

Kelly, Henry Ansgar. "Rule of Thumb and the Folklaw of the Husband's Stick." *Journal of Legal Education* 44, no. 3 (September 1994): 341–365.

Lewis, Jone Johnson. "Rule of Thumb, Not Really: Another Myth of Women's History." About.com. http://womenshistory.about.com/od/mythsofwomenshistory/a/rule_of_thumb.htm (accessed March 5, 2009).

"Origins of 'Rule of Thumb.'" WMST-L File Collection. http://user
pages.umbc.edu/~korenman/wmst/ruleofthumb.html (accessed
April 28, 2009).

Sommers, Christina Hoff. *Noble Lies.* New York: Simon & Schuster,
1994, pp. 203–208.

The Ugly Laws

Boles, David W. "Enforcing the Ugly Laws." *Urban Semiotic,* May 1,
2007. http://urbansemiotic.com/2007/05/01/enforcing-the-ugly
-laws (accessed July 27, 2009).

Schweik, Susan. "Begging the Question: Disability, Mendicancy,
Speech, and the Law." *Narrative* 15, no. 1 (January 2007): 58–70.
Project Muse. http://muse.jhu.edu/login?uri=/journals/narra
tive/v015/15.1schweik.html (accessed September 2, 2009).

Send in the Clown

Dean, John W. *The Rehnquist Choice: The Untold Story of the Nixon
Appointment That Redefined the Supreme Court.* New York:
Touchstone, 2001.

Meso Madness

"Asbestos Lawyers' Scam Pollutes Justice System." *Washington Exam-
iner,* July 21, 2005. www.lucidprose.com/exam_asbestos2.html
(accessed March 15, 2009).

Brickman, Lester. "The Asbestos Litigation Crisis: Is There a Need for
an Administrative Alternative?" *13 Cardozo Law Review 1819–
1889 (1992).* Manhattan Center Institute for Legal Policy: Point
ofLaw.com. www.pointoflaw.com/articles/archives/1992/01/the
-asbestos-litigation-crisis.php (accessed April 1, 2009).

Case Details. "DUI vs. Mesothelioma and PPC's Most Expensive Key-
words." September 17, 2008. U.S. Law. www.uslaw.com/us_law_
article.php?a=301 (accessed April 28, 2009).

Delaney, Kevin J. "Web Startups Vie to Detect 'Click Fraud.'" *Wall
Street Journal,* June 10, 2005. www.whosclickingwho.com/images
-new/wcw-wallstreetjournal.pdf (accessed April 8, 2009).

Giguere, Eric. "Mesothelioma: The One Word Every AdSense
Publisher Knows?" April 18, 2006. Unofficial AdSense Blog:

Independent Advice and Tips About Google AdSense, www
.memwg.com/mesothelioma-the-one-word-every-adsense-pub
lisher-knows (accessed April 1, 2009).

Hodes, William. "Two Cheers for Lying (About Immaterial Matters)."
The Professional Lawyer 1 (May 1994).

Liptak, Adam. "Competing for Clients, and Paying by the Click." *New
York Times*, October 15, 2007. www.nytimes.com/2007/10/15/
us/15bar.html (accessed May 2, 2009).

"Mesothelioma Attorneys." Asbestos.com: The Leading Mesothelioma Cancer Resource. www.asbestos.com/mesothelioma-law
yer/attorney.php (accessed March 9, 2010).

Olson, Walter. "Thanks for the Memories: How Lawyers Get the Tes-
timonies They Want." *Reason Magazine*, June 1998. http://reason
.com/archives/1998/06/01/thanks-for-the-memories/1 (accessed
May 2, 2009).

Taylor, Stuart, Jr. "Asbestos Litigation: Evidence of Massive Corrup-
tion?" *The Atlantic*, December 31, 2003. http://brothersjuddblog
.com/archives/2004/01/massive_corruption.html (accessed April
1, 2009).

Wall, Aaron. "Mesothelioma: Greed, Cancer & Profits." *Search-Marketing
Info*, December 2, 2004. www.articlealley.com/article_414_7.html
(accessed April 8, 2009).

Index

Act of Proscription (England, 1746), 55

Act of Swans (1482), 91

Act to Prevent Maiming and Wounding) (England, 1671), 186–88
    eventual enactment of, 198–200

Act to Prevent the Employment of Female Labour in Certain Capacities, 188

Act to Prevent the Selling of Live Fatt Catle by Butchers (1663), 109

Act to Protect White Labor Against Competition with Chinese Coolie Labor and to Discourage the Immigration of the Chinese into the State of California, 189

Age of Innocence, The (Berkoff), 162

Agneau du Quercy, 143

Agriculture and Markets Law, 106–7

Air Force Sabre Drill Team, 155

Alabama
    deliberate injuries in, 68
    voting in, 61

Alfonso X the Wise, 47

Alice in Wonderland, 28

Alligator, 98
    stealing, 101–2

American Civil Liberties Union, 141, 154–55, 193

Animal rights
    of beavers, 102–3
    of chimpanzees, 110
    in Italy, 90–91
    of lab animals, 110–11

Animals. *See also* Animal rights; Bear; Cat(s); Cows; Dogs; Horses; Mary the elephant; Monkey, Hartlepool; Pigs; Rats; Swan(s)
    companion, 106–7

court trials for, 85–88
    hairdressing of, 91
    Internet hunting of, 155–56

Annoying behavior, 173–74

An Ordinance for Preventing of Mischiefs Arising from Doggs in This City (Philadelphia), 88–89

Antarctica, treaty of, 79

Antarctic Sun, The, 80

Antarctic Treaty, conflicts with, 79–80

Anti-Social Behaviour Act (2003). *See also "Common Scold" (communis rixitrix)*
    adults/children violating, 191

Ant raising (China), 181–82

Arbroath Smokie, 142–43

Archery, 153

Arctic Circle, murders in, 79

Arkansas, horn honking in, 72

Ashtrays, standards/testing of, 205

Asimov, Isaac, 82

Assize of Arms (Ireland), 14–15

Assize of Bread, 7, 10, 12

Association of Masters of Harriers and Beagles, 96

Athelstan, King, 31

Auckland, Local of the New Zealand Electrical Worker's Union, 99

Baker, Norman, 151

Balloon
    releasing, 149
    union rats, 182–83

Balloon Council, 149

Baron & Buss P.C., Texas, worksheet of, 207–8

Barroso, Jose Manuel, 165

Bathing garb, 122

Bawdy Courts, British, 20–21
Bear
    baiting, 153
    wrestling, 103
Beards, 32, 73
Beaurre des Deax Sevres, 143
Beavers, 102–3
Bedding Rule Critical Violation of
    Severity Level III, 168
Bedding stuffings, 167–69
Belbin, James, 51–52
Belford University, degrees from,
    217–18
Bengh, Henry, 131
Bentham, Jeremy, 52–53
Berkoff, Steven, 162
*Best Management Practices for Resolving
    Human-Beaver Conflicts in
    Vermont*, 102–3
Bible, 25
Bicycle riding, 145–46, 163
Bigfoot Travel Center, 141
Big Squirt Candy Spray, 138
Black holes, 76
Blackstone, William, Sir, 181
"Bloody Code" (1700s), 51–52
Bodies, dead
    cremation for, 21
    galvanic process on, 3
    language for, 83
    trade in, 2–3
Body Heat (film), 201
Body thinness, extreme, 163–64
Boechler, Tracy, 89
Boobie pillows, 118
Book of Dooms, The (Ethelberht),
    33–34
Boston Strangler, 213–14
Bouncy Castles, 160
Bower, P. Frederico, 66
Bowling alleys, 152–54
Boycotting laws, 182–83
Braden, Mary, 172–73
Brehan Law, Ireland, 28
Bright Tunes Music v. Harrisongs Music,
    159–60
Britby, John, 6
British Acts, 30
Bronderer, Elizabeth, 6
Brown, John Wayne, Jr., 98
Bullard, D. A., 173
Bullock, Sandra, 150
Bungee jumping ride, reverse, 84
Bunyan, John, 25
Burchill, Julie, 162
Burdine, Calvin, 209
Buses on Screen (website), 150
Bus-spotting, 150–51
Butter, 119

Calamity Jane, 61
California Association of Homeowner's
    Associations, 186
Camel Corps, U.S., 104–5
Canada, 80, 132, 151–52, 179, 208,
    212–13
    beavers in, 102
    North Pole jurisdiction by, 79
    pennies in, 63
    rescue/salvage interference in, 69
    space station laws by, 83
Cannibalism, coincidence of, 136
Capitulary for Saxony, 21–22
Caps, baseball, 141
Carrots, 133, 143
Case of Swans, Trinity Term (34
    Elizabeth I), 92
Cat(s), 60, 125
    talking, 103–4
Catsup, 129–30
Census Bureau, U.S., 148
Cesan v. The Queen, 208–9
Charlemagne, King, 21–22
    Lex Frisionum for, 23–25
Charles, King, Declaration of Sports
    by, 51
Chassenee, Bartholomew, 86
Chastity tassels, 139–40
Cheese
    Roquefort, 142
    in Wisconsin, 119
Chefs, 157–58
Chilingarov, Artur, 79
Chops, 157–58
Christian Coalition, 158
Church of God with Signs Following, 97
Cicero, 54–55
Circuses
    English, 164–65
    jobs for children in, 161
City Council, Chino, California, nuclear-
    free zone in, 70
City street laws, England, 184–85
Clameur de Haro, 211–12
Clinton, Bill, 120, 137
Clothes drying campaign, websites for,
    185–86
Code of Assura, Assyria, 35–37
Codex Hammurabi, Babylon, 3–5
    wisdom of waters in, 4
Codex Theodosianus, 55
Coke, Arundel, 188
Cole, Pat, 173–74
Colonial American laws, 40–42
    "Articles, Laws and Orders" in, 41–42
Commercial Item Descriptions (CID),
    129–30
Commission for the Promotion of Virtue
    and Prevention of Vice, 125

"Common Scold" (communis rixitrix),
    women convicted for, 171–73
Concordat of Worms, 60
*Congressional Research Service (CRS)
    Report for Congress, Declaration
    Procedures* in, 178
Consent to Death, 193
Control of Manufacture and Sale of Food
    Acts, 120
Coots, Gregory James, 98
Cornish Pasty Association, 143
Court of Appeals, U.S., Large Hadron
    Collider in, 75–76
Court Roll, Ramsey, England, bad
    conduct fines on, 6–7
Couwenberg, Patrick, removal of, 203–4
Coventry, John, Sir, 199
Cows, 53–54, 109
    tail dragging of, 89
    tipping of, 89–90
Crane, Phil, 120–21
Crime and Disorder Act (1998), 191
Crime comics, 151–52
Criminal Code (Canada), 208, 212–13
Criminal statutes (England, 1700s),
    51–52
Cross-dressing, 5–6, 26, 27, 121
Crottin de Chavignol, 143
Cucciniello, Alfonso, 115
Cumberland Sausage, 143
Currie, David P., 210–11
Cutpurse, Molly, 26

Dalai Lama, 78
Dale, Thomas, 11–12, 153
Dallamura, Amy Beth, 192
Data, meaningless, 178
Davies, Peter Maxwell, Sir, 92–93
"Dead Hand," 201
Deadwood, South Dakota, laws in, 61–62
Declaration of Sports, 51
"Defendant's Motion to Discharge
    Response to Plaintiff's Response to
    Defendant's Response Opposing
    Objection to Discharge," 202
Defoe, Daniel, 47
"Déjà Vu All Over Again," 215
Delmonico's Grill, 157
Department of Agriculture, U.S. (USDA),
    129–30
Dice/cards, 147
*Dignity of Living Beings with Regard to
    Plants, Moral Consideration of
    Plants for Their Own Sake, The*
    (ECNH), 94
Dogs, 60, 71, 88–89, 93, 125
    DNA data for, 112
    English hunting, 95–96
Dominoes, 147–48

Doody, Winifred, 172
Dougal, Jim, 105
Dreher, Ann, 202
Dress Act (England, 1746), kilts/tartan
    ban by, 55
Drug Trafficking Vessel Interdiction Act
    (2008)
    Bower on, 66
    for semisubmersible submarines, 66
Drummond, John, 19–20
Drummond, Stuart, 101
Duels, sword/gun, Kentucky, 177–78
Durian, 118
Duvall, Gabriel, 210–11
Dyeing, animals, 91, 95

Easterbrook, Frank H., 211
East Sussex Wildlife Rescue, swan
    loitering problem of, 93
Ecstasy, 155
Edict for the Extermination of the Clan
    Gregor, 1603, 19
Edison, Cyrus, Dr., 132
Eggs, rotten, 121–22
Egypt, routine court business in, 8–10
Elizabeth I, Queen, 55
Emergency Management Assistance
    Compact, 177–78
Emerson, Ralph Waldo, 193
*Enlightened Judgments, The: Ch'ing-Ming
    Chi—The Sung Dynasty Collection*
    crisscross maneuvers in, 17
    upside down/inside out in, 16, 17
Ethelberht, King, England, 33–34
European Court of Human Rights,
    76, 110
European Organization for Nuclear
    Research (CERN), 76
European Union, Eurojargon/Eurospeak
    of, 197–98
Extraterrestrial exposure statute, 81

Farquhar, Ian, Fox Hunt Master, 96
FDA. *See* Food and Drug Administration
    (FDA)
Federal Ethics Committee on Non-
    Human Biotechnology (ECNH), 94
Ferret (*mustela putorius furo*), 98–100
    bans on, 98–99
    fanatics (ferrants), 99–100
    work of, 99
Ferret Emergency Response Rescue and
    Evacuation Team, 99
Ferrets Anonymous, 99
Fire Department, New York City, 218
Fischler, Franz, Dr., 143
Fish, royal, 92
Fish Empathy Project, 90–91
Fish/frog legs, hygienic, 127–28

Flirting, 127
Flying saucers, 83–84
Food and Drug Administration (FDA), 125
Food Defect Action Levels, The (FDA), 125–27
Food regulations, EU, 122–24
A Foot of Fudge, A Yard of Chocolate, 138–39
Ford Motor Company, 82
Fortune-telling/palmistry, 77. *See also* Fraudulent Mediums Act (1951); Witchcraft
Foster, George, 2–3
Fowl, noisy, 98
Frankenstein (Berkoff), 162
Frankenstein (Shelley), 3
Fraudulent Mediums Act (1951), 179
Fritchy, Barbara, 172

Galvanism, 3
Gambling, 164
Garlick, Walter, 20
Garratt v. Dailey, 215–16
General and Additional U.S. Rules of Interpretation, 138
General Services Agency, 204–5
Gentoo penguins, 80
Gift certificates, 152
Gill, A. A., 158
Giuliani, Rudy, 100
Golf ball
  damage fund, 165
  explosive, 166
Goodell, Rhoda Lavinia, 196–97
Goodiff, Henry, 27
Gosling, Sarah, 51–52
Grand Forks, North Dakota, City Code Article 1 of, 60
Graunger, Thomas, 87
Greased pig contests, 96
Green, Julia, 173
Green Crab Fencing Program, 61
Greene, David, 158
Griggs, Esther, 209
Guidelines for Robotic Safety (OSHA), 81
Guidelines to Secure the Safe Performance of Next Generation Robots (Japan), 82
Gum, chewing, 120–21

Hagberg, Dale, 156
Hairdressing, of animals, 91
Halverson, Elizabeth, 208–9
Handy, Mary-Pope, 175
Hanging, 2, 25–26, 40
  of animals, 87–88
  of monkey, 100–101
Harem Conspiracy, 9

Harmonized Tariff Schedule of the United States (HTS), 137–39
Harrison, George, 159–60
Harrop, Froma, 185–86
Hartley, Robert, 131
Hatch, Orrin, 15, 158
Haunted houses, 147
Haunted Real Estate: A Primer for Real Estate Agents (Handy), 175
Heath, Lawrence, 20
Henderson, Jacob, 202–3
Henry VI, 117
Henry VII, 167–68
Henry VIII, statute of guest punishment, 15–16
Henwood, Susan, 214
Her Majesty's Court Service, 176
Herodotus, 54
"He's So Fine" (Mack), 159–60
Hickock, Wild Bill, 61
"Historical, Scientific and Practical Essay on Milk, An" (Hartley), 131
HIV. *See* Human immunodeficiency virus
Hodes, William, 207–8
Holden, Thomas, 20
Holdings, Stoam, 214
Hormel, 166–67
Horse Protection Act, 108
Horses, 108
  soring of, 108–9
  speeding law for, 184
  tripping, 89
Hotel fraud, Canada, 179
Houdini, Harry, 195
House of Lords, British (May 27, 1606) acts by, 22–23
Hruska, Roman, 210
Humane Society of New York v. City of New York, 100
Human immunodeficiency virus, 140
Humuhumunukunukuapua (Hawaii state fish), 100
Hunt, Stuart, 192
Hunters, disabled, 156
Hunting Act (England, 2004), 95
Hypnotized person exhibit, 77

Il Romano, 157
Immigration Act (1917), "Asiatic Barred Zone" in, 189
Immuno, 110
Ingram, George, 88
International Harmonized Commodity Description and Coding System, 137
International Space Station, Canadians on, 83
Internet hunting, 155–56
Iron, test by, 31, 34

Jail, juvenile, 213
James Beard award, 157
Japan, 82
Japanese Ministry of Culture, 141–42
Jaywalking fines, Shanghai, 191
Jefferson, Thomas, 216
Jennings, Kathleen, 180
Jillman, Ann, 21
Joliet, Illinois, pronunciation of, 65
Journal of the Plague Year (Defoe), 47
Judgement of the Pillory (1300s), 10
Judges, clothes for, 216–17
Juene, Lucien, Mayor, on flying saucers, 83–84
Jurors, texting/tweeting, 214

Kaskel, Gary, 99–100
Kentov v. Sheet Metal Workers Local 15, 182–83
Kentucky Law Journal, 109
Kerzic, Duane, 151
Ketchup, 129
Khamdouleav, Goussein, 165
Khan, Genghis, Great Yasa of, 49–50
Kilts/tartans, 55
Kirk, Nigel, 96
Kissing, anti, 116–17
"Kissing Capital of the World," 117–18
Knyvet, Edmund, Sir, 15–16

Lacey, Martin, 164
Large Hadron Collider, 76
Las Siete Partidas (The Seven Part Code), Spain, 47–49
  Jews tolerated in, 47–48
Law Code of Gortyn (Crete, 450 BCE), 49
Lawes Divine, Morrall and Martiall, 11–12
  on bowling, 153
Lawn sprinkler, 186
Lawyers
  advertising of, 206–8, 212
  sleeping, 209
  squabbling, 215
  women, 196–97
LeBan, Craig, 157–58
Ledru, Robert, 210
Leeke, Sarah, 172
"Legal tricksters" (China), 16–19
Leviticus, 183
Lewdness/lascivious behavior, 137
Lex Frisionum, 23–25
Lex Salica. *See* Salic law
Libel law (American), 157–58
Liberty and Livelihood, march of, 95
Lillie, Margo, Dr., 89
Liquor still seizures, 150
London Symphony Orchestra, 99
Lord Byron, 27

Louisiana food, 136
Luotonen, Lauri, 150

Maaco Paint Shop, burglary of, 202–3
Maat, goddess, 9
Mack, Ronald, 159
Maden, Patrick, 26
Magtymguly International Prize, 73
Maine, laws in, 60–61
Manteno, Illinois, facial tissue/handkerchiefs in, 70
Mardi Gras Prohibited Throws law, 147
Margarine, 118–19
Marine Worm Tax, 60
Mark, 97
Marks, Rodney, 80
Marriage, 120
Marrow, Ann, 27
Martinez, Emilie, 106
Mary the Elephant, 88
Maspero, Gaston, 9
Massachusetts, laws of, 69–70
Massage parlor uniforms, 139
Masters of Foxhounds Association, 95
Maynard, George, NH motto coercion of, 193
McCaffrey, Rob, 151
McCarthy, Frances, 173
McEntee-Taylor, Carole, 179
McFarland, George, 209–10
McGregor Clan, 19–20
McMurdo Station, 80
Meat, inflated/blown, 140
Melton Mowbray Pork Pie Association, 142
Merritt, Amos, 26
Merseyrail, 180
Mesothelioma Internet subculture, 206–8
Miah, Shamsu, 93
Michigan national anthem, 156–57
Miles, Carl, 103–4
Milk, swill, 71–72, 131–32
Millwood, Thomas, 27
Ministry of Information (South Korea), 82
Modern Prometheus, The. See *Frankenstein* (Shelley)
Monkey, Hartlepool, 100–101
Monoghan, Mary, 172
Monson, Richard, 186
Moore, Tom, Jr., 213–14
Morwinston, Lucy of, 27–28
Moscow State Circus UK, 165
Mr. Potato Head, 138
Mswati III, King, 139
Muppets, 166–67
Muppet Treasure Island, 166–67
Murder Act (1751), 2–3
Music royalties, 149–50

Mustard/Horseradish, 130
"My Sweet Lord" (Harrison), 159–60

Narrative of Arthur Gordon Pym of Nantucket, The (Poe), 136
National Aeronautics and Space Administration (NASA), on extraterrestrial exposure, 81
National Football League, 158
Nature, legal rights for, 94
Nesilin Code, Hittite, 37–39
Neumann, John von, 162
Newgate Calendar, 25–28
New Hampshire
  laws of, 57–59
  motto of, 57, 193
New York City Friends of Ferrets v. City of New York, 99
New York Ferret Rights Advocacy, 99
Nix v. Heddon, 132–33
Nokia, 189
Nonstick coatings, 124
North Pole, 79. *See also* Arctic Circle
  Russia claiming, 79
Nudity, 133–34

Occupational Safety and Health Administration (OSHA), on robots, 81–82
Office of Science and Innovation (England), on robots, 82
Official Methods of Analysis of the AOAC International, 130
Old Man of the Mountain, 58
Ooozy Pops, 138
Ophidiophobic Anti-Snake Online Store, 97
Ordeal by Bread and Cheese, 31
"Order Denying Motion for Incomprehensibility," 202
Orlando Sentinel, 167
OSHA. *See* Occupational Safety and Health Administration

Pact of Umar, Middle East, Christians tolerated in, 48–49
Palendrano, Marion, 172
Pan, Matthias "Hiasl," 110
Pants, low riding, 140–41
Parker, Richard, 136
Patrick (saint), *Senchus Mor by*, 28–29
Peter the Great (Russia), taxes by, 32
Petition from Commons to Be Excused from Kissing the King Because of the Plague, 117
Petition of Commons That Priests Be Pardoned for All Accusations of Rape, 1449, 14
Pet passports, 107–8

Pez Candy Dispenser, 138
Piccoli, Rodrigo, 174
"Picture Our Train" photo contest, Amtrak, 151
Pigs, 86–87
  cooked food for, 90
  greased, 96
  toys for, 105
Pilgrim's Progress, The (Bunyan, John), 25
Pippin the Short, 21
Pizza, Naples rules for official, 116
Plagiarism, 159–60
Plague, 146
  Bills of Mortality on, 46–47
  laws to combat, 45–47
Plants, rights of, 94
Pleas at Lichfield (1200s), iron ordeal in, 34
Pleas at Northampton (1200s), 12–13
Pleas at Wapentake of Aswardhurn, 1200s, 42
Pleas of the Crown (England), "misadventures" in, 39–40
Pleas of the Manor of Abbey, 3
Pleas—The Hundred of Triggshire, 27–28
Plymouth Colony Division of Cattle, 53–54
Pocatello, Illinois, SmileFest in, 64
Poe, Edgar Allen, 136
Poker/gambling, 161–62
Poker Players Alliance, 162
Police and Criminal Evidence Act (PACE), 151
Poltergeists, 175–76
Pork Pie Appreciation Society of Ripponden, 142
Poyser children, 192
Prevention of Terrorism Act (England, 2000), 151
Privy Council (Scotland, 1603), 19
Protected Geographical Indication status, 142
"Protecting What's Right," (Baron & Budd), 207
Providence (Rhode Island) Journal, 185–86
Psychics (British), 178–79
Public Bowling Centers. *See* Bowling alleys
Puritans, 51
"Putting Students Where They Belong," 215

Quahog Tax, 60
Quintana, Leonard, 187–88
Quintana, Shannon, 187–88

Radner, Gilda, 54
Ramses III, Harem Conspiracy of, 9

Rationale of Punishment, The (Bentham), 52–53

Rats, 86, 182–83

Redfearn, Jerry, 97

Reed v. King, 174–75

Rehnquist, William, 206

Reincarnation Application, Tibet, 78

Remembrancia, London, on plague, 45–47

Repeal of the Act Prescribing the Wearing of Highland Dress, 55

Report of the Select Committee of the Board of Health, 132

Report of the Senate Judiciary Committee, 1982, 15

Reptiles, kissing, 108. *See also* Alligator; Snake(s)

Rhode Island, laws in, 63–64

Richardson, Thomas, 20–21

Ridge, Agnes, 20

"Right of Husband to Chastise Wife," 181

Right to Bear Arms, 15

Robertson, Karin, 90

Robot Ethics Charter (South Korea's Ministry of Information), 82

Robots, dangers from, 81–82

Roman Ecloga (800s), 50

Roman laws (200–500 CE), 42–44

Roomba vacuum robots, 82

Roosters, 87, 98, 112–13

Royal College of Veterinary Surgeons, 95

Royal Institute of Technology, Sweden, on robots, 82

Royal proclamations (England 1400–1500), 10–11

Rule Against Perpetuities, 200–201

Ruppie, Bridget, 173

Russkaya Pravda, Russia, 13–14

Rykener, John, cross-dressing by, 5–6

Salic law, 8

Sancho v. U.S. Department of Energy, CERN et al., on Large Hadron Collider, 76

San Diego Paranormal Research Project, 175

Sandys, Thomas, Sir, 199

Sarkozy, Nicolas, 163

"Save Our Ugly Fruit and Vegetables" campaign, 122

Schultze, Elizabeth, 172

Scott, Jack, 149

Sea Moss License, 60

"Security Emergency" (Italy), 174

Senchus Mor, 28–29

1700 York Associates v. Kaskel, 99–100

Shark Finning Prohibition Act, 105–6

Sheep and Goats Order (Wales), 111–12

Shelley, Mary, 3

Silly string sales, 159

Sleeping, in courts, 208–9

Sleepwalking, crimes during, 209–10

Smarties, 139

Smith, Francis, 26–27

Smucker's, jams of, 135

Smyth, Elizabeth "Few Clothes," 20

Snake(s), 141
  charmers, 96–97
  farms, 97
  handling for faith, 97–98
  worship, 97–98

Sokell, Dean, 209

South Carolina, laws in, 64–65

South Pole, 79–80. *See also* Antarctica
  markers on, 80
  violence in, 80

Soviet Republic of Turkmenistan, 72

Spam, reputation of, 166–67

Spanking machine, 52–53

Specter, Arlen, 158

Speed (film), 150

Speeding laws, 184, 189

Spiritual Workers Association (SWA), 179

Sporting exhibitions, 167

Stambovsky v. Ackley, 175

State of New Jersey v. Wayne DeAngelo, 182–83

State Religious Affairs Bureau Order No. 5 (China), "Reincarnation Application" by, 77–78

State v. Rhodes, 180–81

Statute of Apparel, Elizabeth I, 55

Statutes of the Commune of Biella, 35

"Stigmatized Property," 174–76. *See also* Haunted houses
  disclosure laws for, 175–76

Stormfront.org, 15

Sudebnik, Russia, judicial duel under, 13

Sumerian Code, Lipit-Ishtar, rental oxen damage in, 2

Summerford, Darlene, 97

Summerford, Glenn, 97–98

Super Bowl parties, religious, 158

Supreme Court, U.S., 205–6, 217
  trivial justices of, 210–12

Sushi inspector squads, 141–42

Sussman, Gavin, 214

Swan(s), 91–93
  English royal, 91
  loitering, 93
  song, 92
  Upping, 92

Swanning Courts, 91

Swann v. Pack, 97

Swaziland, HIV in, 149

Tarriff Act (1883), 132–33

Tax law, Australia, 196

Tennessee Walking Horse, 108–9
Teosto (Finnish copyright society), 149–50
Texas Court of Appeals, on snakes, 97
Theaters
    ban on, 146–47
    hats in, 148
Theft completion, 210
Thomas, John, 46
Thomas, Mark, Dr., Beagle Master, 96
"Three Laws of Robotics" (Asimov), 82
Tiberius, 116
Todd, Thomas, 210–11
Tokens, 159
Tomatoes, 132–33
"Tongue splitting," statutes, 78
Trainer of the Year Award, 109
Trainspotting, 151
Transue, Hillary, 213
Trousers/slacks
    Cicero on, 54–55
    Codex Theodosianus banning, 55
    Herodotus on, 54
Turkey scrambles, 96
Turkmenbashi, Glorious Father of All Turkmen, 72–73
    eccentric laws of, 73
Twelve Tables, Rome, 32–33
Two Cheers for Lying (About Immaterial Matters) (Hodes), 207–8

Udal Law, 92
Ugly people laws, 183–84
UK Border Agency, immigration applicants to, 164
UK Department of Environment, Food and Rural Affairs (DEFRA), 105
UKTV channel, England, dumbest laws contest by, 67–68
Underwood, Thomas, 25–26
Unfair Commercial Practices Directive, 179
University of Chicago Law Review, 210–11
Unlawful Internet Gambling Enforcement Act, 161

USDA. *See* Department of Agriculture, U.S.
Utah, laws in, 71–72

Vanjoki, Anjssi, 189
Vermont, laws in, 67
Vermont's Energy Act (2009), 186
"Vexatious litigants" (England), 176–77
Vidal, Gore, 145
Virility, sexual, 132

Walking Horse Trainers Association, 109
Warner, Neville, 105
Washington, Henry, 97
Watson, Graham, 143
Weather Bureau, fake weather reports and, 66
Weeks, Trevor, 93
West Virginia, red/black flags in, 70
Wheelie Bins, bugging of, 190
Wifebeating, 35–36, 180–81, 187–88
Wild Creatures and Forest Laws Act (1971), 91–92
Wildlife Protection Act (India), 96
Williamson, John, 26
Winter, Rowland, 45
Wisconsin food statutes, 119–20
Wisconsin Historical Society, 119
Witchcraft, 80
    Act (1735), 179
    by animals, 87
Wood, Joseph, 25–26
Woodburne, John, 187
World Customs Organization, 137
Wort, ballings of, 128
Wrestling
    bear, 103
    fake, 154
Wrigley's, 121
Wrobel, Leopold, 192
Wurde der Kratur (account to be taken of the dignity of living beings), 94

Yew, Lee Kuan, 120

Zhendong, Wang, 182

About the Author

Nathan Belofsky is an attorney practicing in New York City.